STOCKTON-SAN JOAQUIN COUNTY LIBRARY

W9-CPV-323

WITHDRAWN

50¢

3 NOV '61
2 MAY '69
APR 5 '65
12 OCT '68

616.89
S765c

C.2

Spotnitz, Hyman, 1908–
    The couch and the circle; a story of group psychotherapy.
[1st ed.] New York, Knopf, 1961.

274 p.   22 cm.

1. Group psychotherapy.   ɪ. Title.

RC488.S65   616.8915   61-7121 ‡‡

The Couch
and the Circle

The Couch
and the Circle

A STORY OF
GROUP PSYCHOTHERAPY

B Y

HYMAN SPOTNITZ

M.D., MED.Sc.D.

New York : *Alfred · A · Knopf*

1961

616.89
S765c
c. 2

L. C. catalog card number: 61–7121

THIS IS A BORZOI BOOK,

PUBLISHED BY ALFRED A. KNOPF, INC.

Copyright © 1961 by Hyman Spotnitz. All rights reserved. No part of this book may be reproduced in any form without permission in writing from the publisher, except by a reviewer who may quote brief passages in a review to be printed in a magazine or newspaper. Manufactured in the United States of America. Published simultaneously in Canada by McClelland & Stewart, Ltd.

FIRST EDITION

PUBLIC LIBRARY

SEP 5 1961

STOCKTON, CALIF.

T O

My Patients and Students

Teachers all

Preface

THE RELATIVELY NEW and rapidly developing field of group psychotherapy—its origins, methods, importance, and future—is the subject of this book. It was written to acquaint the layman and the specialist in allied fields with the nature of this form of treatment. Possibly, the book will also help some readers prepare for the reality of the experience.

In responding to the need for a non-technical exposition of group treatment, I have been aware of a keen desire to share the enthusiasm and interest kindled by my practice with the general public. Written in this spirit, the book subordinates theoretical concepts and techniques to impressions of human beings working together. I have focused primarily on the words and feelings of those who search for new meanings to old experiences and re-direct their lives through corrective relationships formed within the therapy circle.

Strictly speaking, it should not be necessary to explain my many references to the patient on the couch who com-

municates privately with his analyst. The twosome, though
designated as "individual" in the terminology of psychotherapy, is also a group. Moreover, it is permeated with the
unseen but deeply felt presence of other persons, mentioned or unmentioned, who have influenced both partners
or will themselves be influenced by the results of the therapeutic process.

But the principal reason why both forms of treatment
are encompassed in this book is more personal. I began to
write it solely in terms of my experiences in group psychotherapy, but found it impossible to convey the reality of
these experiences without relating them to the allied
science which led me into the field. In my thoughts as in
my practice, individual and group treatment are inextrica-
bly linked. I have endeavored to clarify their common de-
nominators and intrinsic differences.

Directly or indirectly, all of my patients figure in the observations I record. Between our first meeting and our fare-
wells, their feelings and behavior underwent an infinite
variety of changes. To trace their transformation in detail
was not possible, but I have tried to give characteristic
glimpses of their emotional development by indicating how
they appeared to me at various stages of our relationship. I
have also revealed what went on in my own mind while I
treated them, my thoughts and feelings about them, and the
objectives which shaped my own communications.

Nevertheless, the ethical requirements of medical confidentiality and the protection of my patients have been accorded priority over the reader's enlightenment. I have
carefully disguised the external realities of their lives to
safeguard their anonymity, while preserving as faithfully
as possible the flavor and integrity of their personalities.
The same emotional problems dominate so many cases that
several persons may suspect that they are the subject of
each story I relate. The fact of the matter is that many in-

dividuals have undergone similar experiences and have made parallel disclosures in the course of treatment.

Some patients I write about were extremely complex personalities suffering from mixed and, in some cases, grave psychiatric disorders. I have described them as simply as possible. Though a pattern of behavior may have been determined by hundreds of different factors, I have tried to meet the demands of elucidation and brevity by emphasizing those which were outstanding within the context of the case. In other words, explanations were oriented to clarity rather than scientific comprehensiveness.

The shortcomings of the book are my own. Its virtues, whatever they may be, reflect the efforts of many persons. I would acknowledge, first of all, an indebtedness beyond measure to outstanding teachers who prepared me for my clinical practice and research pursuits and to those, too, who have illustrated for me in a personal way the workings of the mind in sickness and in health—my patients and students.

I had willing assistants among colleagues, friends, and relatives. Their careful reading of the manuscript at various stages yielded valuable criticism and suggestions.

I am grateful to my editor, Henry Robbins of Alfred A. Knopf, Inc., for his stimulating guidance. I benefited from his encouragement and remarkable patience.

To Julia Older Bazer, I am greatly indebted for editorial assistance in the organization and preparation of the text. She lightened the formidable task of making professional material comprehensible to the lay reader and worthy of printer's ink.

Contents

Part · I : INTRODUCTION TO THE GROUP
SETTING   *1*

  1 My First Group   *3*
  2 The Third Psychiatric Revolution   *22*

Part · II : THE ANALYTIC TREATMENT
PROCESS   *53*

  3 The Phantom Figure   *55*
  4 Themes with Variations   *87*
  5 Patients and Treatment Settings   *107*
  6 An Afternoon in My Office   *138*
  7 "Whatsoever I Shall See or Hear"   *164*
  8 The Meaning of Recovery   *191*

Part · III : THE PSYCHOTHERAPIST   *223*

  9 A Group Psychotherapist in the Making   *225*
 10 Some Group Leaders Talk Shop   *243*
 11 Looking Ahead   *262*

Part · I

INTRODUCTION TO
THE GROUP SETTING

[1]

◇◇◇◇◇◇◇◇◇◇◇◇◇◇

My First Group

"ARE YOU a psychoanalyst or a psychotherapist?" a patient asked me the other day. The answer, that I am both, perplexed him, so I went on to explain that psychoanalysis is just one form of psychotherapy. Frequent questions of this sort have made me aware that many people are confused by the overlapping and crisscrossing of professional identities among psychotherapists. I shall therefore start out by clarifying my own status.

Who am I, professionally? A physician whose specialty is psychiatry, the science of treating mental diseases; a psychiatrist who devotes himself to the practice of psychoanalytic psychotherapy. To complete the identification, I am one of a small but rapidly growing number of psychoanalysts who began their careers in individual practice and now conduct groups as well. The name commonly applied to the group treatment we give, one of various forms which were introduced in this country during the first half of this century, is analytic group psychotherapy.

I like to work with one patient at a time, and I like to work with a group. These are basically different procedures, but, in my opinion, both are needed. Some persons require individual treatment; others do better in a group.

And some need both experiences—combined treatment. I became convinced of that fact some years ago when a thin, sandy-haired man, one of my most difficult patients, announced to his group: "I feel cured, folks, so I'm saying good-by. Thanks for all you've done for me. I can look after my family and business from here on without any more trouble, and they can look after me. So I'm ready to pull out of here."

Years have passed since Donald made that statement, but I have good reason to remember it. I was accustomed to hearing such expressions from persons in individual treatment, but he was the first of my patients to declare his psychological independence in a group and thank other patients for helping him achieve it. All the more momentous, he was telling the group something he had not told me during his ten years in and out of intensive individual psychotherapy.

I had formed the group—my first—two years earlier for Donald and several other patients whose cases appeared to be at a standstill. In their new therapeutic alliance, they were joined by a man who had been in individual treatment with one of my colleagues. These were the allies—psychological intimates once a week in my office and total strangers outside—whom Donald thanked.

Feelings cannot be accepted as the sole measure of recovery. He did not think and act at that time like the entirely well person he felt himself to be. Nevertheless, to "feel cured" is a vital ingredient of cure in the severe kind of illness from which he suffered. The group setting gave me an impressive demonstration of its value when it produced that feeling in Donald. He had balanced precariously during his thirty-odd years on the borderline between neurosis and psychosis.

His emotional insecurity at the time he entered the group was baffling, for he had made considerable progress during the decade he had been coming to me intermittently for individual treatment. He had never been hospitalized, and his acute anxiety states were already past history. Yet there was a residue of anxiety which he seemed unable to deal with, even though he realized how unnecessary it was. He also demonstrated a need to be defiantly selfish, to have his own way about everything, and to obtain approval for feeling and acting as he did. At the other extreme, he still tended to be emotionally withdrawn.

Compared with the problems which had already been overcome in his case, the man's inability to become a more sociable human being seemed to be rather insignificant. However, it also seemed to be an insoluble difficulty. He was like a traveler who bogs down indefinitely just a few miles short of his destination after covering thousands of miles on schedule. Even more frustrating was the realization that what was keeping Donald bogged down was his way of life.

He revolved monotonously in a constricted orbit: the apartment which he shared with his wife and small daughter and the office shared with his business partner. Small as these settings were, Donald could always find something going on in them to blow up into at least a low-grade worry. Painful memories of his parents' violent quarrels, which had made his own childhood miserable, intensified his fears that his little girl was being damaged by his constant bickering with his wife. Blaming himself for it, he asked again and again why, now that he was so much better, he seemed bent on ruining his daughter's life. That was a familiar refrain in his sessions.

To Donald, "going out" meant accompanying his wife to a neighborhood movie, where they were as isolated a twosome as if they had remained at home. He had no friends and did not belong to any social groups or professional associations. Understandably, because of his prolonged illness, he had never cultivated a skill or hobby; he did not know how to "let off steam" in outdoor sports. When I pointed out that he might enjoy fishing or watching a good baseball game, Donald asked: "Why do you waste my money talking about sports?"

Unable to acknowledge that outside activity would tend to make him less tense and irritable at home, he insisted that he had to solve his immediate problems before he would have energy to spare for "non-essentials." He was clearly unwilling to tolerate the anxiety of learning to function properly in social situations.

The female members of my first group also seemed unable to weave themselves into the fabric of society. Though they, too, had made substantial headway in overcoming the acute problems which had brought them into treatment, I thought of these four women as refractory patients. Each hesitated fearfully on the threshold to a better life, like a person who has regained his sight through a delicate operation but cannot be persuaded to open his eyes and look about him. For a different reason, each woman seemed disposed to make a permanent crutch of treatment.

Deborah, for instance, was a vivacious young secretary who hated to spend an evening at home, yet rarely left it outside her working hours because of her dread of having an epileptic seizure in public. Home, however, was not much of a haven for her. She was constantly being provoked into arguments by her mother and sisters; they had always treated her as their inferior. Deborah had made marked improvement during five years of individual psychotherapy. This, combined with anti-convulsant medicines, had kept her free from seizures for more than two years, and the symptoms of her earlier functional disorder had practically disappeared. But, as long as the bitter family quarrels associated with her earlier attacks were apt to begin again, therapy seemed necessary for her. New interests and activities and some understanding friends would have helped to counterbalance the harmful effects of the dissension in her home; but her fear of being similarly stigmatized in other settings made her hesitate to expose herself to new dangers.

The progress of Faith, a lonely drinker, was also retarded by a strong fear of being disgraced in some social situation. A librarian in her early thirties, she was a quiet woman with a timid smile who had been trained from infancy to live alone. The only child of a school superintendent and his unloving wife, she had been brought up in a small New England community. Both parents had frowned on any display of emotions. Faith was so accustomed to keeping to herself that, when she fell in love with a married businessman, it was not difficult for her to keep their relationship secret. During his frequent absences from the city, however, she began to rebel against loneliness. In one lone bout with it, she discovered that the companionship of the bottle was relatively safe and far outweighed the pleasure of being with people. For this and other reasons, she became addicted to alcohol. That was one of the problems which brought her into treatment.

She projected her own strong disapproval of her sex life and drinking on those who invited her to join them in various social and professional activities. Cutting herself off from all unnecessary ties was essential, in her opinion, to keep her skeletons from breaking out of her personal closet and threatening her career. Although she had made great progress in treatment and no longer drank compulsively, she seemed to regard her weekly therapy sessions as a sort of perpetual antidote to loneliness amid the ups and downs of her life. Without them, or some other emotional gratification, it was possible that she would become a compulsive drinker again.

When I began to practice psychoanalytic psychotherapy, I had requested my colleagues to send me patients whom they considered to be untreatable. I wanted to find out why they were regarded as hopeless cases and to investigate whether they would respond to newly developed methods. Helen and Edith were among the patients sent to me for this purpose.

A cultured and attractive brunette in her mid-thirties, Helen had suffered for years from severe anxiety attacks which caused her to roll on the floor, grovel, and shiver. She had once attempted suicide as a way out of this suffering. Her first few acute attacks had coincided with her breaking off of her successive engagements to marry. Her last suitor, turned down on the eve of their planned wedding, had brought her to a psychiatrist. After treating Helen for some months, he decided that he could not help her, and challenged me to take on the case of the "terrified virgin." He expressed the opinion that she would never overcome her fear of sex relations, "but please let me know if I am wrong."

Two years later, after falling in love with a handsome naval officer, Helen decided to have an affair with him. She insisted that this was the only way to test her conviction that she would never find a man with whom she was sexually compatible. The affair proved to be mutually satisfactory, and eventually she lost her terror of sexual intercourse. I sent her first psychiatrist this message: "The gates have been stormed."

For reasons of her own as well as her lover's, their affair did not lead to marriage; but Helen had no more acute anxiety attacks, and she became a much happier person. She advanced in her teaching career and functioned capably as head of household for her sick father and mentally retarded brother. When we investigated her tendency to vegetate at home during her leisure hours, however, Helen complained that her slightly crippled arm pained her whenever a social appointment was in the offing. This pain seemed to be connected with her continuing anxiety that acquaintances would shun her if they found out about her physical disability. Her undue sensitivity about a condition which was scarcely noticeable would have yielded in time to new interests and the right kind of friends; but it was difficult for her to make the effort necessary to cultivate them.

Edith, a severely depressed widow in her forties, was described as "hopelessly sick from the year one" by an associate who had examined her in a New York hospital. I administered psychotherapy to her there; she also underwent shock treatment. Even her responses to drugs indicated that this slight, sorrowful woman was a mixed-up creature. For example, her blood pressure went down instead of up when she was given adrenalin. Later, she was referred to me for private treatment. During the next six or seven years, Edith got along tolerably well in her clerical job and took care of her mentally ill father in his last years. She was hospitalized only once—briefly, at her own request, during my first summer vacation after her treatment sessions started, when she felt unable to maintain her equilibrium without them.

As far back as she could remember, she had reproached herself for living. Her mother, who had almost died in giving birth to Edith, mentioned this so often that the tiny girl felt wholly responsible for her mother's suffering. She reacted similarly to the death of her husband. Several other relatives died suddenly in the course of her therapy, and she blamed herself for each death. Life often seemed to be caving in around her, driving her anew to thoughts of suicide.

Although any expression of hostility depressed her in the early stage of treatment, Edith eventually became able to accept it from me without feeling overwhelmed. The knowledge that she was being exposed to hostile feelings as part of the therapeutic process, she said, prevented her from suffering "100 per cent." Still, her fear of being hurt or deserted by others to whom she might become attached made her unwilling to go out socially.

In my dissatisfaction at the slow progress of these five patients, I reviewed their cases and life histories together. Despite substantial differences in their backgrounds and psychiatric disorders, their cases were in two respects strikingly similar. In their years of individual psychotherapy, these patients had never unfolded a memory or dream of a group experience which had aroused feelings of pleasure or excitement. Personal circumstances and illness had helped to mold them into "one relationship" people; that is, their thoughts and feelings, when not focused on themselves, tended to be overcharged with the significance of one other person. Hence, they had become more and more isolated from the stream of normal social activity.

That fact, by itself, was not too significant. "One relationship" and even "no relationship" people stream steadily through the offices of psychotherapists, and the majority of them emerge without undue difficulty into more satisfying lives. The final phase of their therapy and the leave-taking itself are not unnecessarily prolonged, as a rule, because they have relatives and friends at hand to wean them from the old life patterns and draw them naturally into pleasurable social activities. In psychotherapy even more than in other forms of treatment, environmental circumstances beyond the therapist's control and people he never meets may decisively influence the outcome of his cases.

But none of these patients was in regular contact with sociable people. That was the second common factor in these cases, and it appeared to be more serious than the first. They lacked opportunities and incentives for changing their one-to-one patterns of association.

When I reviewed these cases twelve years ago, I was consulting psychiatrist to the Jewish Board of Guardians, a New York child-guidance agency where therapy groups were conducted for children and also for parents. S. R. Slavson, who has played a historic role in analytic group therapy, directed group treatment at the agency. Some of the psychiatric social workers, psychologists, and psychiatrists who consulted me there discussed the personality changes going on in members of their groups. Slavson especially aroused my interest in group therapy as a field of research. I studied the reports published by other analytically trained therapists about the groups which they then conducted rather experimentally. Information obtained from these sources about the social values of the group experience suggested a fillip for my own sluggish cases.

Why not bring these people together regularly to interact in my presence and with my assistance, I asked myself. Might this training not instill them with the extra confidence they needed to begin grappling with the potential stresses of bona fide social situations? After undergoing their first experiences of this sort in familiar and trusted company, like the child who enters kindergarten for the first time clinging to his mother's hand, they ought to be better able to cope with such situations without anxiety.

Acting on that hypothesis, I formed my first therapy group to serve as a bridge between individual treatment and independent social functioning. That was the group to which Donald two years later—and for the first time in twelve years—expressed the feeling that he could go on living without psychotherapy.

From the start, I was surprised at the ease with which my five problem patients adjusted themselves to meeting together. I had expected their first session to be a period of painful feeling-out; but they seemed more comfortable than when alone with me. They obviously felt that it was safe to reveal themselves, and readily accepted each other as fellow patients of mine. This bond and their long conditioning in individual therapy accounted for the unexpectedly comfortable shift in treatment settings.

After introducing them by their first names, I had little more to do. In a relatively relaxed and informal way, they talked frankly about difficulties which they concealed from their daily associates.

Donald followed up my brief introductions with this statement: "I am trying to break my 'worry habit.' It makes me fearful all the time."

People always sized her up critically, said Helen, and she had to behave the same way. "I feel terrible about doing it," she added, "and I am trying to find out why."

Faith declared: "I hated my mother, and now I hate my work."

"I am an epileptic," were Deborah's first words.

Donald and Helen spent considerable time exploring their anxieties together. They tried to demonstrate how helpless they were, as if to say: This is what I want you to help me with. When Donald remarked that he could make anxiety out of any situation, Helen said: "I'm the same way. Sometimes I get chills when I talk to people. When I go shopping, I always expect something horrible to happen to me."

Edith was the last to parade her defectiveness. "I don't blame you people for not speaking to me. It's my own fault, of course."

"We have been respecting your silence," said Donald. After that, he did most of the talking. He made me squirm by flagrantly misquoting me or by distorting some of my comments on his emotional difficulties. He ridiculed me without his usual self-consciousness. He had been so friendly and respectful in the preceding months that I was startled by this new attitude. As I checked my impulse to counterattack and analyzed his behavior, it was difficult not to betray how I felt. But I realized that his great craving for admiration and need to exhibit superiority in the situation unconsciously forced him back into the almost forgotten role of the son trying to overthrow the father.

Indeed, for a man who had often asserted that women always bored him "except at bedtime," he was amazingly gallant and attentive to his female co-patients during the first few group meetings. They were impressed with his daring as he tried to unseat me in their affections. In Deborah's fantasies during the opening session, she told us later,

Donald was a "secret psychiatrist" who was present to assist me in treatment.

With the advent of the sixth group member several months later, Donald acquired a peer rival with whom he repeated this provocative behavior. Jack, a husky man with an air of uncertainty about his movements, was a thirty-six-year-old homosexual. He was admitted to the group at his therapist's request after doing poorly in individual treatment. Donald took it as a personal affront when the women laughed at Jack's wisecracks.

Two hours of group interaction every week introduced some strikingly different experiences into the lives of these people. As I studied their behavior with each other, I recognized the acute needs which individual treatment had failed to meet. The analyst working alone with a patient can provide him with emotional experiences similar to those with a mother or father during the early years of life. It is much more difficult in the one-to-one relationship to create for a patient the emotional validity of being with several brothers and sisters or playmates; and the members of this group had a particularly great need to experience just such a situation.

Faith opened one session with the statement that she had disgraced herself when she was six years old; the memory troubled her. She described a Flag Day ceremony, conducted by her father in the school assembly hall, when she had been called on to recite a stanza of "The Flag Goes By" by Henry Bennett. She knew the poem by heart, she went on, but at the appointed moment, she had been unable to utter a word, or even to stand up. Vividly recalling her father's mortification, she said that she wanted to make amends at once. She then stood up with a great deal of dignity, faced the group, and, with the air of a model child, recited these lines:

> *Hats off!*
> *Along the street there comes*
> *A blare of bugles, a ruffle of drums;*
> *And loyal hearts are beating high:*
> *Hats off!*
> *The flag is passing by!*

It was plain to see that the delivery of these few lines lifted a massive burden from her mind.

His group experience brought Donald many special satisfactions. For instance, his co-members underestimated the severity of his illness; this was heartening for him. I was accused of maligning him when I warned the group that he wasn't as self-confident and well mannered as they took him to be at the beginning.

Later the point of my warning became clear. When he felt completely at ease with the women, he became a fountain of obscenity, spouting out all the sexual feelings that stirred through him during the give-and-take of the sessions. He shocked them by saying that he ought to be able to "neck with anybody I want anywhere," and Deborah punched him for calling her a "good lay." The trouble with them, he complained, was that they couldn't accept the notion that people had "low level" needs.

A series of perverse ideas which he expressed were discussed in the sessions; this was gratifying to Donald. The willingness of the other patients to comment frankly on these ideas reduced his anxiety about having them and made it easier for him to accept the frustration of not acting on them.

The women studied him, analyzed his dreams with more or less psychological sophistication, and made suggestions about his family and business. They advised him to get on better terms with his wife. He was astonished when Faith and Helen both told him that they found him physically attractive. He benefited especially from Faith's influence and affection, which he reciprocated. They enjoyed talking about getting together outside the sessions, but successfully resisted the temptation to do so out of concern for their own improvement.

Donald's dramatic announcement that he was cured was not accepted at face value. It launched an investigation of his behavior. He was called on to give evidence of his improvement and to report what his wife and business associates said about it. His co-patients also gave their own impressions of his conduct. Impatient as he was to leave, he then accepted the group's verdict that he required a somewhat longer period of interchange in a controlled situation to overcome some remaining difficulties and to stabilize the progress he had already made. One year later Donald "graduated" from the group with the enthusiastic consent of its members and the approval of his wife and partner. This marked the close of one of my most challenging cases.

To her co-patients, Helen's improvement was more impressive than Donald's. She outshone them in the early sessions, speaking fluently and with few signs of anxiety. Then Donald complained that her "perfectionistic attitude" inhibited him, and she burst into tears; after that, she talked about her problems with more feeling. On the whole, however, the ease and rapidity with which she adjusted herself led to a meteoric career in the group. In less than six months, she announced that she was entirely well, and she

could not be persuaded that she was overconfident. About
a year after she had left the group so impatiently, she realized that she required further treatment. An associate to
whom I referred her gave her individual psychotherapy
until she recovered.

The group experience helped its other members, to a
varying extent, to live more satisfying lives. Even Edith,
the depressed widow, who joined the group on my say-so
and then tried to prove that she was too sick for it, derived
some benefit from her brief participation. Though too
prone to read rebuff into each attempt of her companions
to respect her silence, Edith spoke feelingly about her emotional problems on several occasions. On resuming her
individual treatment, she gently reminded me that she had
joined the group against her better judgment. Then she
added: "You see, I was right after all." For the first time,
in all the years I had known her, she reproached someone
beside herself. That was her first triumphal moment. Exposure to the other group members' less reverent attitudes
to me had made it possible for her to enjoy it.

During his first six months in the group, Jack showed
marked improvement. He gradually developed an interest
in his co-members, especially Faith. He found himself vying
with Donald for her attentions during the sessions. Jack
told the group that she was one of the few women who
had ever attracted him sexually. He couldn't understand
this because she reminded him of his dead mother, for whom
he still retained deep hatred. His distress about the warmth
of his feelings for Faith turned to panic when the group
began to discuss the possibility of their marriage. The increased anxiety, depression, and revengeful feelings that
would accompany any real effort to abandon his homosexual way of life and permit himself to become more

attracted to women were too threatening for Jack to talk about. He pulled out of the group. Had he remained and discussed his emotional difficulties further, I believe that he would have succeeded in overcoming his fright at the thought of disclosing his hostile feelings. To the best of my knowledge, the group experience ended his treatment.

Deborah did not communicate as freely in the presence of other patients as she had in her sessions alone with me, but the unaccustomed consideration they gave her sharply boosted her morale. The fact that businessmen and professional women enjoyed her company helped her get over her feelings of inferiority. From the first session on, she talked frankly about her epileptic condition; later she began talking about going on dates. Not long after the group ceased to function, Deborah moved out of the city. She found work to her liking in another community, where she had her own apartment and found sympathetic friends.

The treatment experience which transformed Faith from a lonely woman into the group belle was not her last; but it led to marked changes in her attitudes and way of life. The realization that she had made a major contribution to Donald's recovery brought her self-esteem and, apparently, stimulated an interest in "doing good." She became active in philanthropic work and joined a women's club. She found that she enjoyed being with people. She stopped referring to her neighbor's children as "little psychopaths."

It isn't customary, I know, for psychotherapists to refer to the effects of their treatment experiences on themselves; but they enjoy no immunity against psychological change and, indeed, often benefit from it. The day may yet come when they will evaluate the psychological impact of a treatment process on themselves as well as on their patients. It might also be helpful for patients to give their opinions on the emotional development of those human instruments to whom they entrust themselves.

I believe that my first group experience was as significant for me as for my patients—significant for me personally in making me feel more secure in other group situations, as well as professionally in introducing me to an exciting new field of practice and research. Functioning hour after hour as a shadowy figure in a dimly lit room with one patient at a time shuts out a lot of living; that is one of the occupational disabilities of the psychoanalyst. In the group, I felt much more of a human being—a more sociable and lively one. The situation was more challenging. It required qualities of leadership as well as technical skill and the ability to keep track of several lines of communication at a time. Yet the brighter atmosphere and more spontaneous emotional processes were at one and the same time more relaxing and more invigorating. The dramatic spirit of the interaction, the repartee and the intensity of the feelings coming to the fore made more of me come alive in the group sessions. I became aware, too, that the feeling of being revitalized often carried over into my individual treatment sessions.

The healing value of the understanding which one patient gives another in the group greatly impressed me. Strength of personality and favorable traits which had not been delineated in extended individual treatment revealed themselves in various group situations. I found myself less concerned with the causes of illness and basic pathology than with the current functioning and social resources of each patient.

Among analytic psychotherapists today, there is vigorous disagreement about the relative efficiency of individual and group procedures and about many other aspects of these

two treatment experiences. Most practitioners would probably agree, however, that the analyst who has been trained
exclusively in individual psychoanalysis is bound to experience certain anxieties about his ability to function in the
group setting. I recall my own uncertainty and feeling of
insecurity in the few minutes before my first therapy group
assembled for its opening session.

It had been easy enough to create the new setting for
their treatment. The couch had been removed, and a semi-
circle of chairs faced the desk. But how about me? Could
I transform myself just as effortlessly into a group therapist?
In retrospect, I suppose that the entirely new situation ahead
of me gave rise to a fear of the unknown. I had never felt
so unprepared before an individual analytic session, even
during my first weeks of practice, because I had some personal experience and training to guide me. Until I became
familiar with the countless maneuvers which go on in
individual analysis, I would think back to what my own
psychoanalyst or control analysts would have done in one
eventuality or another. But I had no previous personal
knowledge of the group setting. I wondered if I would be
able to provide the difficult patients I was bringing together
with a truly therapeutic experience.

Would I know how to sustain the simultaneous impact
of several diverse and complicated personalities? Would
I invariably be able to keep track of what would be
going on, let alone analyze and respond appropriately?
Would my inexperience and insecurity about my change
of status be sensed by my patients? And would I know how
to draw the line between suitable control and overprotec-
tion?

In the years that have passed since I asked myself those
questions, the uncertainties which beset me before my first

group session have been dispelled. Some of my questions were answered by the group experience which began that same evening. Many more answers emerged out of other therapy or training groups. Some of these groups I conducted myself; others I observed from a distance, like a deeply concerned but unseen godfather, in the capacity of consultant psychiatrist to their respective leaders.

What I have learned, what I have observed, and what I have experienced in the course of these activities is the substance of this book.

[2]

◆◆◆◆◆◆◆◆◆◆◆◆◆◆◆

The Third Psychiatric Revolution

WHEN I STUDIED ANATOMY as a medical student, I was surprised to learn that firsthand knowledge of the structure of the human body, the foundation of modern medicine, was not available to physicians until the last few centuries. Many of their earlier notions about the causes and effects of disease processes on the body seem very far removed from our present understanding.

Their ignorance of the body was nurtured by the superstitions and mystical beliefs which long hampered medical training and treatment. Until the fourteenth century, students were forced to rely on descriptions of the human anatomy written by Galen, a Greek physician of the second century, or later writers who copied his descriptions, because the dissection of the human body was regarded as an act of sacrilege. When it was finally permitted, medical schools were allowed few cadavers for demonstration purposes; usually they were permitted to hold one annual dissection, the corpse being that of an executed criminal. Vesalius, the founder of modern human anatomy, stole a body from the gallows for one of his investigations.

Before Vesalius, whose textbook of human anatomy was published in 1543, anatomical dissections added little significant knowledge of the detailed structure of the body and the relation of its parts. It was easy for me to understand why this was so when three drawings of anatomical dissections, illustrations from the texts by Vesalius and two of his predecessors, came to my attention.

These drawings vividly suggest how anatomy finally emerged out of the Dark Ages. In the earliest, a professor of medicine sits on a dais reading to the assembled students from the medical bible—Galen's textbook on anatomy—while his barber-servant dissects a cadaver some distance away. In the second illustration, an instructor directs and demonstrates while the servant wields the scalpel; but here, too, the professor is perched on his dais expounding from Galen. To handle the corpse was still regarded as beneath his dignity. In the third drawing, from the title page of the historic work of Vesalius, neither dais nor textbook is in evidence. The professor himself stands over the cadaver dissecting, explaining and referring to an articulated human skeleton close at hand.

This was the kind of dissection which led Vesalius to the astounding discovery that Galen himself had never dissected the body of a man. What had been studied and accepted for nearly fifteen hundred years as faithful descriptions of the human organism was actually based on the dissection of monkeys, pigs, and goats. The earlier ideas about the body which were not supported by such direct observations were abandoned; and we gradually acquired

our present knowledge of the relation between bodily structure and functioning and how one influences the other.

In psychiatry, too, we have moved closer to our data
and abandoned many distorted ideas about the anatomy of
the mind and how it operates. With the introduction of
group psychotherapy we acquired a new vantage point
from which to investigate the dynamics of human behavior.

In some respects, the development of psychiatry as a
medical science has paralleled that of anatomy. The popular
superstitions and religious prohibitions which retarded
scientific knowledge of the body's structure also helped to
preserve the mysteries of the mind. Mystical notions about
evil spirits, like those about dead spirits which interfered
with the study of the cadaver, kept the mentally ill outside
the pale of general clinical medicine during the first two
thousand years of its history. Abnormal mental states were
not regarded as illness due to natural causes but as evidence
that an evil spirit had entered the body. The person afflicted
was in the grip of some witch or demon.

By and large, all that the ancient world offered him was
the incantation of a witch doctor or sorcerer designed to
drive the evil spirit from his body. In the Middle Ages, the
deranged were thought to be sinners in Satan's clutches,
and their treatment—to misuse the word here—was zealously applied with torture racks, branding irons, or bon-
fires at the stake. They were sinners, they were criminals,
and the evil spirits in them had to be punished. They were
shackled and set apart from the community like loathsome
and dangerous monsters.

These notions linger on. As a boy, I often heard people
described as being possessed of the devil or "born wild."
Some parents try to "beat the badness" out of children who

misbehave. The psychiatrist's understanding of bad behavior as related to illness or faulty training is still not fully accepted.

The first glimmer of recognition of this idea in modern times came during the sixteenth century, when a few physicians imbued with the humanistic ideals of the Renaissance spoke out against the superstitious approach to mental illness and the cruel treatment accorded its victims during the Inquisition. Men like Paracelsus, Vives, and Weyer sparked a crusade for the abolition of restraints and for compassionate treatment of the mentally ill which eventually brought them within the province of medicine. This movement, which has come to be known as the First Psychiatric Revolution, received dramatic expression in Paris in 1793 when Philippe Pinel struck off handcuffs and anklets from the inmates of the Asylum de Bicêtre. The men he freed had been chained to dungeon posts as long as thirty or forty years.

The approach of Pinel and others like him was dominated by an entirely new concept: Mentally ill people needed kindness and would respond to it. Perhaps the evil spirits which troubled them had resided in the bodies of their tormentors. Physicians brought into the mental institutions were urged to project themselves into the situation of their patients, and manage them through persuasion instead of force. Pinel and his associates introduced the practice of taking a detailed history of each case. The patients proved to be more amenable to kindness than to the treatment provided. It consisted chiefly of bloodletting, cold baths, salves, and emetics. Physicians then believed that they were dealing with one illness.

Slowly they came to recognize that these patients suffered not from a unitary illness but from different kinds of disorders. Their description, classification by symptoms, and the early efforts to understand their causes marked the beginning of the Second Psychiatric Revolution. It culminated with the discovery by Freud and others that certain forms of illness described by Emil Kraepelin could be cured. But kindness alone wouldn't help these patients. They also needed understanding and close study—treatment on an individual basis.

Within the traditional framework of the doctor-patient relationship, a new form of treatment—scientific psychotherapy—developed during the nineteenth century. It was administered to the less severely afflicted in private consulting rooms and community clinics. Systems of psychotherapy based chiefly on suggestion were the first to be employed; one of these was hypnosis, an important byway explored by Freud. More intensive systems developed later, based on appeals to the reason and will power of the patient, on his emotional bond with the physician, and on the liberating effects of the act of confession. Later Freud discovered the importance of the emotions and childhood experiences in the development of illness. His investigations of the irrational aspects of the personality—the unconscious —ushered in the most intensive form of psychotherapy: psychoanalysis.

When Freud and his collaborator, Breuer, treated a neurotic patient, it became apparent to them that his illness resulted from memories connected with his experiences with persons of significance in his past life, especially his mother or father. The treatment situation tended to reactivate his problems, so that the analyst could usually find out what they were and what was needed to heal them.

I was aware of these discoveries as a medical student, but only because I read psychoanalytic literature. In my psychiatry courses thirty years ago, I heard nothing about these findings. I was taught that some mental illnesses were caused by brain damage and that the cause of others was unknown. The belief was current that persons suffering from conditions of uncertain origin also had defective brain tissue, which would be proven with further refinements in microscopic research.

Discussion of Freud's microscope of the mind was rarely sanctioned in academic circles at that time. Few university professors suggested the possibility of using an instrument as controversial as psychoanalysis, or that one might be able to find out the cause of an illness and alleviate it just by listening closely to a patient and analyzing what he said. Since then, however, the concept that detailed study of one person by another is therapeutic in some cases has permeated psychiatry.

Later it became evident that the treatment twosome created practical difficulties. Its time-consuming nature was frequently pondered. The analyst underwent long, rigorous, and costly training and then had to limit himself to a few patients. Each of them required so much time that he could not help many others who needed his services. For those he helped, on the other hand, treatment was costly. Was there some way out of this dilemma, some way of reconciling the patient's need for lengthy study and the analyst's social responsibility to help a larger number?

These and other issues confronted other practitioners, among them physicians treating physical and psychosomatic illness, psychiatrists in the mental and general hospitals and community clinics, and representatives of the other helping professions. While some of them were primarily concerned with helping more people, others sought easier or additional ways of dealing with their current cases.

Here and there, for their own purposes, these various practitioners started to treat patients in groups. Good results were reported, often better than were expected or could be accounted for. A body of theory developed to explain what happened in this form of treatment. And finally, psychoanalytic studies of how group members affected each other led to the recognition that their joint presence was beneficial; the group was a therapeutic force in its own right. Moreover, observations of the spontaneous functioning of people in therapy groups brought new understanding of the general nature and effects of human interaction—in family and numerous other groups—which can be applied in the interests of society at large.

This, in essence, is the significance of what has come to be known as the Third Psychiatric Revolution.

As a reported method of treatment, group psychotherapy originated in this country, the scene of most of its early history. In 1905, Dr. Joseph Hersey Pratt of Boston organized the "home sanatorium treatment of consumption" at the outpatient clinic of the Massachusetts General Hospital. His weekly meeting with indigent patients, which he called a class, was admittedly a timesaving device; and his brief inspirational talks were given to help them repress their pessimistic thoughts and to keep them in treatment. The young physician, whose teachers of medicine had included Osler and Welch, knew that recovery from tuberculosis depended as much on what goes on in the head as in the chest.

The group meeting itself got scant notice in Pratt's earliest reports; he regarded it at first as no more than a pleasant social hour. He stressed the physical improvement of those who adhered to the prescribed regimen, and explained how they could live an outdoor life in the slums. This meant sleeping in improvised porches, shacks, or tents pitched in back yards or on tenement roofs. One patient, refused permission to use yard or roof, slept with his head sticking out of a window.

"It should never be forgotten that it is the individual, not the disease, that needs treatment," Pratt told the Johns Hopkins Medical Society in 1906. "We have been fortunate in having a small class, and so we have come to know our patients not simply as 'this case of fibroid phthisis' and 'that of pyopneumothorax,' but as 'Elmer and Patrick.' "[1]

Pratt later attributed the spirit of camaraderie which developed among these patients to their "common bond in a common disease." He went on to say: "The testimony of a star patient exerts a powerful influence on the newcomer, but the healthy appearance of most of the patients probably makes a deeper impression than anything that is said."[2]

Another reason for the remarkable success of this program was suggested thirty years later by Dr. Richard C. Cabot in a statement commemorating Pratt's sixty-fifth birthday. Cabot, who had watched Pratt conduct the class in its early years, observed that his hopefulness and buoyancy, joined to his natural liking for all sorts of people, made him a "very powerful therapeutic instrument." In Cabot's opinion, the class members persisted in treatment to please Pratt and improved "not wholly because they wanted to get well but largely because he wanted them to, —a very queer and very human state of things."[3]

Pratt's original class continued for many years, with

[1] Joseph H. Pratt: "The 'Home Sanatorium' Treatment of Consumption," *The Johns Hopkins Hospital Bulletin*, Vol. XVII (1906), p. 140.
[2] Idem: "The Principles of Class Treatment and Their Application to Various Chronic Diseases," *Hospital Social Service*, Vol. VI (1922), p. 404.
[3] In the *Anniversary Volume* issued by the Lancaster Press in 1937, p. xxvi.

little change in its operations, and was a model for many others. The same approach was adopted by other physicians, including psychiatrists, for the management or supplementary treatment of persons with physical or psychosomatic conditions. One early group was composed of undernourished children, to whom gaining weight became a game. Over the years, physicians have obtained good results from regularly bringing together patients with chronic conditions like diabetes, heart disease, hypertension, peptic ulcers, rheumatism, and obesity. In groups small enough for members to get to know each other, it has been found that their mutual encouragement and rivalry facilitate their emotional adjustment to the condition and stimulate their co-operation in treatment.

Pratt himself, although active in other fields of medicine, continued to work with groups and acquired a more psychological orientation. In his "thought-control class," formed at the Boston Dispensary in 1930 for patients with functional nervous disorders, he addressed himself to their mental attitudes as well as their physical symptoms. He no longer encouraged patients to suppress worrisome thoughts and feelings, as in his first tuberculosis class; indeed, members of his later group were stimulated to admit their problems. The force of his own personality continued to be an important element of the treatment, but his approach became less authoritarian. Pratt commemorated the fiftieth anniversary of his first group less than a year before his death.

The policy of grouping patients with psychosomatic conditions whose weighty medical charts testified to repeated visits to a clinic was adopted by other physicians. For example, Dr. Samuel Hadden introduced similar groups more than twenty years ago at the Philadelphia General Hospital.

"We wondered why the patients had returned repeatedly to clinics which had not helped them," said Dr. Joseph J. Peters, who now directs the group program at the hospital. Often they returned with fresh physical symptoms, probably because the clinic helped to satisfy their emotional needs. When they were permitted to remain in a group after becoming symptom-free, Dr. Peters continued, they transferred their dependency to the group and their symptoms were often alleviated.[4]

Some general hospitals have been sufficiently impressed with the results of group treatment for outpatients to extend it to bed patients. At Mount Sinai Hospital in New York City, the first group was formed in 1945 for women with menopausal complaints who, years after their physiological symptoms had subsided, haunted the gynecology clinic, apparently to socialize with other clinic visitors. The thirteen members of this group, the oldest of whom was sixty-five, identified with each other in airing feelings of isolation and guilt about their vague physical complaints. They came to understand their emotional difficulties and developed new social interests. All of these women improved considerably, and their visits to the clinic ceased or markedly diminished. In 1952 staff psychiatrists introduced groups and group techniques in the treatment of hospitalized patients. A "morning therapy group" has replaced early rounds on the psychiatric wards, according to Dr. Aaron Stein, who directs the hospital's diversified group therapy activities.

From the National Hospital for Speech Disorders in New York City, Dr. James Sonnett Greene first reported in

[4] From the *Proceedings of the Second Annual Institute of the American Group Psychotherapy Association*, New York, 1958, p. 32.

1935 on his group treatment of stutterers. He called this "open door" psychiatry. Stutterers passing his open office door were called in to join those being treated inside. He brought society to the stutterer, to overcome his fear of social contacts, Greene said.[5] Other types of "work groups," devoted to the solution of some common problem, were formed later, in institutions and other settings.

While Pratt, the internist, was stimulating the development of medical group therapy, others who figure in the early history were more directly concerned with emotional illness and social maladjustment. Psychiatrists began to work independently with groups for different reasons; generally, they were unaware of each other's theories, methods, and findings.

One of these pioneers, still active in the field, is Dr. Jacob L. Moreno. His name is identified with non-analytic treatment, and notably psychodrama. This is a widely used form of action therapy based on his experiments with various social groups in Vienna before World War I. The cathartic effect of the drama, which Aristotle observed more than two thousand years ago, are exploited in psychodrama and other therapies based on spontaneous interaction.

Moreno introduced the terms *group therapy* and *group psychotherapy*, though he first used them, in 1932, in a tangential connection: to describe a system of grouping prisoners so that their interactions would be mutually beneficial. About twenty years ago, these terms became a sheltering blanket for the many strange bedfellows in the field.

Alfred Adler was probably the first psychiatrist to carry on systematic class discussions on mental hygiene in a school guidance clinic. He did not envisage himself as de-

[5] In *The Journal of the American Medical Association*, Vol. 104 (1935), p. 2242.

parting from the individual method of treatment when he counseled a child in Vienna in the 1920's in the presence of adults—physicians, teachers, and others studying his procedures. However, their presence had a favorable effect on Adler's relationship with the child. This type of counseling is therefore regarded as a sort of group psychotherapy or, more precisely, group guidance. Rudolf Dreikurs, who conducted groups of alcoholics in Vienna in 1928, introduced Adler's method of family counseling to the United States. He and other Adlerians are enthusiastic exponents of group treatment.

In the mental hospitals early in this century, groups were assembled primarily to make it easier for psychiatrists to influence the inmates. Dr. Austen Riggs lectured to his patients over a loud-speaker at his sanitarium in Stockbridge, Massachusetts. Initially, this approach was designed to explain the patient's problems to him and, by appealing to his intelligence, to prevail upon him to overcome them.

Later the lecture method was employed for a different purpose and with different results. Psychiatrists in various institutions became concerned about the poor morale of their patients, their lack of social interests and of stimulating activities. The need to counteract their isolation and emotional withdrawal, and to arouse their confidence in recovery, led to the introduction of another kind of group therapy.

Its earliest reported use was in St. Elizabeth's Hospital in Washington, D.C. In 1918 a young psychoanalytically oriented staff psychiatrist received permission to give a series of lectures to groups of war veterans confined to the wards for schizophrenics. Dr. Edward W. Lazell spoke to them in simple language about their war experiences and the causes and symptoms of their illness. Though some of

them seemed lost in fantasy or mumbled to themselves
while he was talking, he observed that men who had been
described as "unreachable" patients absorbed much of what
he told them. "Silent, dreamy boys suddenly became interested and drank in every word, realizing that here was
someone who understood their troubles," he reported later.[6]
In his opinion, the eventual recovery of some of these
men was initiated by these lectures. Later in his career,
Lazell conducted similar lectures for psychotic patients in
other mental hospitals.

Dr. L. Cody Marsh was influenced by Lazell but lectured
more informally. A minister and morale officer in World
War I before entering the field of psychiatry, he employed
techniques which he described as the "psychological equivalent of the revival," without its terminology or religious
objectives. He worked with severely disturbed patients at
Kings Park Hospital, New York, and later at the Worcester
State Hospital in Massachusetts.

Marsh worked for the emotional stimulation of his patients through lectures, discussions, stunts, roll calls, singing
and dancing to the music of an ancient phonograph. The
development of a group bond through principles of crowd
psychology, morale-boosting, soul-winning, and salesman-
ship, he said, made it easier for him to "sell sanity" to members of a group than to a solitary patient in his office. His
groups, averaging less than twenty patients, met in a small
basement room. Marsh regarded each patient as a "student
who has received a 'condition' in the great subject of civili-
zation" and therefore required re-education.[7]

He organized group activities for hospital personnel and

[6] In *U.S. Veterans' Bureau Medical Bulletin*, Vol. VI (1930),
p. 733.
[7] In *Mental Hygiene*, Vol. XV (1931), p. 347.

relatives of patients, and attempted in various ways to interest the community at large in their rehabilitation. Stressing the social and environmental aspects of mental illness, he adopted the credo:

> *By the crowd have they been broken,*
> *By the crowd shall they be healed.*

Many who conduct groups today share this treatment philosophy. Marsh probably did not realize that he was dealing with emotionally starved adults, but he intuitively sought to give them the psychological nourishment they needed.

The importance of measures to reintegrate the hospitalized patient into society was stressed by others who worked in the mental institutions during the 1930's. Dr. Jacob M. Klapman took a more didactic approach than Lazell and Marsh, whose experience he was unaware of when he began grouping psychotic patients for treatment. To counteract their easy distractability, he developed a system of pedagogical therapy employing textbooks, scripts, or lectures on various aspects of social adjustment. Group members took turns in reading aloud from these texts. The method was designed to stimulate emotional release and the objective discussion of problems; and the leader played an authoritarian role. Klapman and other directive psychiatrists also administered such treatment in their private practice.

Another Chicago psychiatrist who worked with the most seriously disturbed patients, especially after their discharge from mental hospitals, was Dr. Abraham A. Low. He developed a system of group therapy known as willtraining, which was used chiefly in the Midwest. This approach was based on the notion that the spotting of verbal errors—

"self-sabotage"—helped a person to talk and perhaps, therefore, to think more sensibly. Brochures and a regular newsletter, "Recovery News," were circulated among Low's group members, who formed an organization of their own. Similar bodies, among them Resurgo, founded by Klapman, have developed out of the therapy groups conducted in the mental hospitals.

Among the first few psychiatrists to apply psychoanalytic principles to the treatment of groups in the mental hospitals were Dr. Louis Wender and Dr. Paul Schilder. Their reports on these groups during the thirties influenced the main stream of development to a much greater extent than those of Dr. Trigant Burrow, who is now recognized as the first American psychoanalyst to practice group therapy. A pupil of Freud who later developed a social theory of behavior which he called phyloanalysis, Burrow's first reports on his private practice of "group analysis" were published in 1924, six years after it had started. He and his students analyzed each other in experimental groups of from four to twenty members. Burrow emphasized the social aspects of neurotic disorders. His group activities were oriented primarily to social research rather than therapy.

Wender started to work with groups in 1929 at a New York mental hospital, after observing that patients entering the hospital responded well to group living. He found that some of them did much better in groups than in individual therapy. They identified with each other and became more objective about their own difficulties. He also pointed out that the group setting stimulated more spontaneous communication, with the subsequent release of anger and resentment. Wender regarded the group as a family unit and maintained his fatherly interest in its members after they were discharged from the hospital.

Schilder conducted groups at Bellevue Hospital in New York City; his first reports on them were published in 1936, four years before his death. A powerful therapeutic instrument himself as well as an outstanding authority on psychoanalytic techniques, he worked out analytic procedures for his groups which were later adopted by other therapists. Although he considered individual psychoanalysis to be the more efficient method, he pointed out that his patients often experienced powerful emotions and disclosed significant information in the group which they had been unable to reveal when alone with him. Schilder came close to recognizing that the group itself was a therapeutic force.

During the thirties, analytic group therapy also made its appearance in the general community. It was first utilized chiefly in the treatment of disturbed children in the child-guidance clinics. Several distinct practices were introduced, employing activity or play exclusively in the treatment process or in combination with interviews. The name most prominently associated with these therapies is that of S. R. Slavson, who is responsible for many of the theoretical concepts, methods and techniques of analytic group therapy. Some of them developed out of his experimental work with problem youngsters at the Jewish Board of Guardians, where he became director of group therapy in 1934.

Slavson abandoned a career in civil engineering because he decided that he was less interested in working with steel and concrete than in building healthy personalities. "A child is a wonderful thing," he once said. "It can do incredibly amazing things if you create the proper situation. And it can be distorted terribly if you create and maintain the wrong situation."

His contributions to group therapy are, in essence, a fusion of his experience in progressive education and recreational group work, which began in 1911, and his personal psychoanalysis during the twenties. One of the few non-medical pioneers who was analyzed before entering the field, he transplanted psychoanalytic principles to the group setting, using them as the basis for his extensive theoretical work in the field. In the face of inertia and active opposition, he trained psychiatrists, psychologists, and psychiatric social workers to conduct groups. Like others today who are primarily interested in its scientific advancement, Slavson has tried to discourage the use of group therapy for reason of expediency. He has frequently warned that it is not a cure-all.

Young people in Slavson's earlier school and recreational groups had been encouraged to do creative work in painting, music, literature, and other arts. This program was designed to help them discover their talents through their own activities. Slavson volunteered his services to assist the Jewish Board of Guardians in developing a similar program for its clinics. This was therefore introduced, not for treatment purposes, but for what was called creative activity or "therapeutics of creative activity."

What went on in the earliest clinic groups puzzled Slavson. The youngsters made unimpressive use of the art and handicraft materials provided; nevertheless, significant changes for the better were taking place in their behavior. If what they fashioned was not of sufficiently high quality to have effected the personality improvements they displayed, to what should these be attributed? A thorough analysis of one year's records of the sessions of one of these groups led him to the conclusion that many interactions among the children had been of therapeutic significance. It became clear to him that the group situation itself had been a factor in the therapy. Various other curative aspects of the collective functioning were identified later.

Slavson has told me an interesting story in connection with the reorientation of this program. Having satisfied himself that it was therapeutic rather than creative activity, he suggested that the agency's program should be called *group psychotherapy*. He thus informed his brother, John Slawson, at that time the director of the Jewish Board of Guardians. The latter advised Slavson that psychiatrists might think it presumptuous for lay therapists to describe their activities in medical terminology. The agency program was therefore referred to as *group therapy*. He was not aware that Dr. Moreno had already used both terms, a few years earlier, in publications on prison procedures. Slavson, as far as is known, was the first person to use them in their current sense.

Activity group therapy, which was introduced on a regular basis in the clinics in 1934, is widely used today with young children. They are encouraged by an "unconditionally loving," permissive therapist to discharge their pent-up feelings symbolically through play, arts and crafts, sports and similar activities. Hence, activity replaces words as the medium of communication. Each child interacts with the other children present and forms the type of relationship which he himself wants with the group leader.

During the next five years, Slavson and his associates experimented with other procedures. As experience indicated that some children were either too disturbed to function well in activity groups or needed a setting more conducive to the expression of their thoughts and feelings, the activity-interview procedure was introduced in 1937. Play group therapy for preschool youngsters and interview group therapy, first used with adolescents, were introduced in the next two years.

Slavson's natural gifts as a group leader were put to a grueling test in 1935. When he discusses his early experiences in the field, he is fond of recalling a riot which took place during the summer of that year at the agency's residential center for delinquent girls at Hawthorne, New York. For six weeks they had been in a state of hysterical rebellion. Because their own attendants and the state police had been unable to restore order, he was asked to take whatever measures he thought were necessary.

Driving out to the institution with two assistants and an assortment of materials for group activities, he found that the girls were confined to their rooms behind locked doors, with all windows barred. He invited them to come to the staff lounge later in the day. The teen-agers complied, out of curiosity and because the lounge had been forbidden territory for them; but for two hours Slavson was hooted and jeered every time he tried to address them. He faced them good-naturedly and bided his time. Finally one of the ringleaders silenced the gathering and called out: "Let's hear what the mug has to say."

He thanked the girls and told them he respected them for fighting for their rights; he often had to fight for his own. They were asked to present their complaints, and these were all recorded and given serious consideration. Slavson told the girls that he trusted them. He was asked to prove this by turning over the keys to the main entrance of the building. The keys were handed over. They were returned, unused, the next day. The doors were then unlocked and the window bars removed.

Though there were probably deep-seated causes for the riot, according to Slavson, the strict disciplinary measures instituted by the center's new director had sparked a great deal of emotional tension. She was asked to leave immediately. Slavson remained at Hawthorne for a year, introducing group procedures for therapeutic purposes as well as educational and recreational activities. There were no more riots.

The unplanned and often accidental start of many early therapy groups is reflected again in an account by Betty Gabriel of the genesis of the first activity-interview group. Mrs. Gabriel was one of the first psychiatric social workers to practice group therapy. As she reported in 1939,[8] she had been holding office hours twice weekly in a neighborhood center some distance from the guidance clinic with which she was affiliated. Her hours at the center became generally known and children began to drop in without appointments. Mothers also came to consult her, sometimes bringing in sisters and brothers of the youngsters who were then in individual treatment at the center.

Reluctant to turn away her visitors, Mrs. Gabriel held impromptu meetings for them from time to time. She talked informally with the children about their home and school problems; they also played games together and put on puppet shows. Eventually these gatherings were turned into weekly therapy meetings, combining activity and interviews, for seven boys and girls with serious emotional problems.

The room where they met had a movable wall. The little group members often helped Mrs. Gabriel manipulate it to allow more space for their activities. She sat in a corner

---

[8] In *American Journal of Orthopsychiatry*, Vol. IX (1939), pp. 146-69.

of the room, recording as unobtrusively as possible what went on. The children joked with her about her notes and occasionally helped her decipher them.

In 1941, Dr. Lawson G. Lowrey, an outstanding figure in child psychiatry, was commissioned by the Jewish Board of Guardians to assess its group-therapy program. After making a critical analysis of the records for nineteen groups and a follow-up study of the 101 cases sampled, he concluded that good results had been achieved in 70 per cent of the cases.

Pointing out that the basic tenets of therapy by the group had been carried out, Dr. Lowrey stated: "The children do recognize the similarity to a family group, making such comments as 'you are my new father,' 'this is just like a home.' The group does offer opportunity for the child to have those positive experiences which have been missed in the past. . . . It is clear that group therapy works best for deprived, frustrated and infantilized children. To the extent that it can adequately substitute for the deprivations, free the frustrations and give opportunity for growth and maturation of the individual child, group therapy is a successful and economical procedure." [9]

Among the first adults to enter community therapy groups were parents of children treated in the guidance clinics. The earliest parent groups were treated at the Brooklyn Child Guidance Center in 1939. The system of therapy developed by Dr. John Levy, which combined analytic and educational techniques, was employed.

In embarking on the treatment of parents, the objective of the child-guidance clinics was to prevent them from interfering with the therapeutic progress of their children.

[9] From the late Dr. Lowrey's unpublished survey. See *American Journal of Orthopsychiatry*, Vol. XIII (1943), pp. 648–90.

Treatment designed specifically to help parents form more understanding relationships with their youngsters has developed over the years into the so-called "child-centered group guidance of parents." [1] This form of consultation has been rather widely employed for parents whose children suffer from the same type of emotional problem or organic illness—for example, schizophrenia, epilepsy, or cerebral palsy.

Parents in the groups at the child-guidance centers often evolved treatment goals of their own, sometimes voluntarily and sometimes as a result of the more direct approach to their own unconscious conflicts. This was the practice of group therapists at the Brooklyn Child Guidance Center, who turned parents of some of the children in treatment into clients themselves, often unwillingly at the start. Generally, however, it was found that mothers and fathers who insisted that their children were the problem came to recognize the desirability of effecting some change in their own personalities.

The steady but slow development of group therapy in both institutional and community settings seems placid indeed when one compares it with the emergency boom initiated by World War II. This, paradoxically, was what brought the new treatment method to the knowledge of the general public. But while the layman hailed it as expedient and less expensive than individual treatment, its rather slapdash use during the war and the extravagant claims made for it in some quarters made group treatment unpalatable to many practitioners. Ironically, they labeled, it "wonder medicine." Group therapists are "sailing in rather big boats on the waves of science," wrote Dr. Ernest Harms in 1945

[1] S. R. Slavson: *Child-Centered Group Guidance of Parents* (New York: International Universities Press; 1958).

in the journal *The Nervous Child*. It took more than a decade to retrace the steps that led to this public espousal during and immediately after the war emergency and to build the structure of group psychotherapy on a firmer foundation.

The use of group psychotherapy on both the war and home fronts was officially sanctioned. General George C. Marshall recommended its use to army psychiatrists. Dr. William C. Menninger, as director of the army's psychiatric service, circulated a manual on group procedures to military establishments. A meeting of the National Research Council in 1944 on group therapy and its applications gave further impetus to such treatment for civilians as well as for those in military service.

To the United States War Department, group psychotherapy was "any procedure which tends to improve the mental health of more than one individual." [2] Lecture courses, inspirational talks, classes, and films for groups running into the hundreds were common; so were classes and discussions, some conducted by the patients themselves. "Gripe" sessions for the ventilation of feelings proved helpful. Explanation, re-education, exhortation, and group hypnosis were employed. There was also analytically oriented treatment. Some of it was patterned after methods which Dr. S. H. Foulkes and other British psychiatrists had developed with impressive results in their military treatment centers.

Efficient management and rehabilitation of psychiatric casualties were major goals of the group therapists in the various war theaters. With a caseload of an estimated 900,000 patients, more than one third of whom were discharged from active service on psychiatric grounds, mili-

[2] War Department. *Technical Bulletin*. No. 103 (1944), p. 7.

tary psychiatrists had to handle these casualties as rapidly as possible. Experience dictated, too, that the men be treated as close to the combat zone as possible. Admittedly, group therapy was recommended because not enough therapists were available to give individual treatment.

"A discussion of the relative value of individual and group psychotherapy in the Navy is absurd," wrote Dr. G. N. Raines and Dr. L. C. Kolb from the Norfolk Naval Hospital in an article published in a psychiatric journal in 1944. Military organizations which worked, played, lived, and fought as a group had no other choice than to be treated in a group.

The magnitude of the task confronting the psychiatrist and his inadequate preparation for it was suggested in a postwar report by Dr. Robert E. Peck. In 1943 he was one of three staff psychiatrists treating seven hundred psychiatric patients in an army general hospital in North Africa. For most of the cases, the choice was simple: group psychotherapy or no psychotherapy. The former was selected largely because the soldiers seemed to benefit from their own bull sessions in the wards.

"My previous experience with group therapy consisted only in an interest in it while attached to a state hospital," Peck wrote. "At that time I had surveyed the literature and had some idea of the various techniques then extant. I also had a few months' practical experience with it in treating psychotics. This seemed of very little help in the job I faced in North Africa." [3] Although the first groups were unsatisfactory ventures, he reported getting better results when he carried on the same kind of treatment in Italy.

This experience was characteristic. In all of the combat

[3] *International Journal of Group Psychotherapy*, Vol. 1, (1951), p. 365.

areas, psychotherapists learned how to treat groups while in the process of treating them. They improvised, tested out, and exchanged techniques as patients suffering from battle fatigue, acute anxiety states, hysteria, concussion headaches, and other disturbances streamed into the base hospitals from the battle fronts.

Members of groups formed in 1943 for evacuees from the South Pacific and Mediterranean combat zones spoke in simple language and often with intense feeling about their experiences in foxhole and jungle. They were encouraged to talk after a few sessions, but not forced to do so. After hearing others talk, with the group leader making occasional interpretations, men who had been unable to discuss harrowing experiences in individual interviews began to disclose their turmoil and fears. The airing of a succession of similar and yet dramatically different problems built up a pattern of common experience which enabled each participant to view his own difficulties more objectively.

Not infrequently, he also gained insight into the mainsprings of the current disturbance. One soldier recalled his timidity, as a schoolboy, about fighting other boys. His acute worry that he had showed cowardice under fire was relieved when two other group members disclosed their own childhood fears of neighborhood bullies. To cite another example, a soldier who had collapsed after seeing his buddies die in one bloody engagement told his group how, as an eight-year-old, he had witnessed the accidental death of his favorite cousin.

As experience accumulated in the military installations, other values besides the saving in time and money emerged from group treatment. Where individual psychotherapy was also available, both forms were used with greater discrimination, and comparative evaluations were possible. Some psychiatric casualties who had not responded to individual treatment did better in groups; the reverse was also true. The study of behavior and attitudes in group sessions was found to provide a more reliable guide to diagnosis and the screening out of persons unfit for military duty than the impression of a single observer. Group treatment, it was also agreed, eased social adjustment and the rehabilitation of men transferred to non-combat duty.

Among the most seriously ill men, returned to military hospitals in this country, group therapy resulted in a marked improvement in morale. Merchant seamen suffering from "convoy fatigue" or the aftereffects of a torpedoing also were treated in groups, as were psychiatric casualties in other war-related services.

Since the war, group therapy has been instituted on a regular basis in the country's military hospitals, including Walter Reed Hospital in Washington, D.C. In the hospitals of the Veterans Administration, extensive research in group treatment has been conducted by Dr. Florence Powdermaker and Dr. Jerome D. Frank.

On their return to civilian life, many psychotherapists who had worked with groups in military settings entered private group practice or became affiliated with similar treatment programs in hospitals and social agencies. Predictions that patients consulting private practitioners would be hostile to group treatment proved unfounded, on the whole.

Statistics on the growth of the professional literature tell an impressive story of expansion and, notably, of the enormous impact of World War II on this form of treatment. From 1906, when Pratt's first report on his class method appeared, through 1939, about 125 papers were published. During the next decade more than four times that number of items were added to the professional literature, including several books on theory and practice. As the year 1959 drew to a close, the bibliography of group psychotherapy contained more than 2,000 entries, the majority of papers being the clinical reports of hundreds of group practitioners. An estimated 200 reports now appear annually, most of them in the professional journals in the field.

Some of the papers published are more distinguished for their enthusiasm and originality of concepts than for their scientific value. There are numerous case histories—mostly "success stories"—but little information on treatment process, which is admittedly difficult to explain. Though many psychotherapists use methods which are relatively similar, their respective theoretical concepts make them appear to be far apart. One of the common complaints in the field is that there are as many group techniques as there are practitioners.

In individual psychotherapy, too, the numerous approaches, methods, and levels of intensity make for considerable confusion. This is aggravated by semantic difficulties. Despite his intense preoccupation with communication processes, the psychotherapist finds it difficult to convey clearly the nature of his own activity. To give an example of a procedure is often easier for him than to describe it in terms which will be comprehensible to his colleagues, let alone the general public. His subjective view of his own activity may range from the notion that he is dispensing therapy as scientifically exact as mathematics or as organic as a drug, to the impression that what he is creating for his patients is an aesthetic living experience.

The average therapist regards his procedures as an

amalgam of scientific and artistic elements, but tends to stress those which reflect his own approach and temperament. At one recent professional meeting, forty different definitions of *psychotherapy* were proposed. Our as yet very incomplete understanding of many factors which contribute to mental illness also encourages a great divergence in therapeutic activity.

But the introduction of the group setting has created a new tower of babel. More than twenty-five methods were discussed in one recent textbook.[4] In addition to methods I have mentioned, there are others employing drama, music, puppets, blackboards, or drawings, as well as so-called leaderless methods, multiple psychotherapy, the self-help method, round-table therapy, and hypnotherapy.

The great diversity in concepts and modes of treatment is probably inevitable, in view of the erratic development and conflicting approaches to this new therapy—still a makeshift to some and to others a scientifically valid form of treatment whose systematic development has scarcely begun. Nevertheless, there are indications that the over-all picture is becoming less complex. Some of the methods devised are already outdated or fast becoming so. Some were employed for special purposes, notably research. Others, like the lecture methods, are now used only rarely outside the mental institutions and will continue to decline as group practice becomes stabilized. Groups small enough to permit their members to communicate with each other in the interests of desirable personality change are the keynote of the future.

Close study of people in all sorts of interaction, from the tiniest unit—the twosome of patient and therapist—to

[4] Raymond J. Corsini; *Methods of Group Psychotherapy* (New York: McGraw-Hill Book Company, Inc.; 1957) pp. 57-83.

the foursome and larger aggregates conventionally known as a therapy group has shed new light on behavioral problems; this knowledge in turn has greatly influenced the course of psychotherapy. Treatment based primarily on suggestion, repression, inspiration, coercion, and support has given way to analytic systems which reflect our growing understanding of unconscious processes. From the latest evidence available to me, covering psychiatrists treating groups in private practice, it appears that four out of five employ an analytic approach. This means that, regardless of the divergence in their concepts and procedures, they analyze the behavior and statements of each patient, giving him explanations which eventually produce a comprehensive and integrated account of his functioning as a total organism.

The phenomenally rapid development of group psychotherapy has taken it into many new fields. There are few settings where it is not used today, few problems to which it has not been applied. Its growth in many parts of the world, largely in the wake of its organized development in this country and, more recently, in England, is probably unparalleled in the annals of the healing arts.

The psychotherapist now makes direct observations of the mind in action in two excellent laboratories. One of these is especially well equipped to penetrate the cause-and-effect relationships which govern the personality and to learn how it interacts with one other person. The other laboratory is a more lifelike matrix. It brings the mind into sharper focus as an apparatus engaging in many different kinds of relationships, and possesses valuable devices for scrutinizing its simultaneous interactions at home, work, and generally in social situations. The first laboratory, of course, is individual psychoanalytic therapy; the second is analytic group therapy.

There are about as many different points of view about the second laboratory as there were about the first a generation or more ago. Some psychotherapists are of the opinion that the first laboratory has been superseded by the second; others consider the second to be an inferior substitute for the first.

I disagree with both these points of view. As I continue my practice, the needs of my patients not only take me into newer channels of activity but also prevent me from abandoning either of the treatment settings created by the second and third psychiatric revolutions. Both seem to me to be crucially needed—as well as the other psychotherapeutic laboratories which will be opened in the future.

Part · II

THE ANALYTIC
TREATMENT PROCESS

[3]

===

◇◇◇◇◇◇◇◇◇◇◇◇◇◇◇

===

The Phantom Figure

A YOUNG WOMAN beginning her third month of psychoanalysis lodged an odd complaint the other day as she was leaving my office. "Maybe I shouldn't tell you this," Rose began rather diffidently, "but I'm afraid something must be wrong with this analysis. It's giving me such a wonderful feeling. People say you're supposed to suffer, but so far my sessions with you have been very enjoyable. Maybe I'm having too good a time. Are you sure you're treating me correctly?"

This was pleasant to think about during the brief interval before my next session. Since Rose was making good progress so pleasurably, was I not entitled to think of myself as a pretty good doctor, and an agreeably therapeutic personality to boot? Something about me did seem to affect people favorably, I mused, and they benefited from my friendly manner.

But this mood of self-exaltation ended with the sound of my doorbell. The patient who followed Rose would certainly not echo her sentiments. Quite the contrary. For many months Hector had bemoaned every hour spent with me. Admittedly, these "visits to hell" were leading to a marked improvement in his relations with his family and business associates and in his physical health, too. The asthma which he had been certain was incurable no longer bothered him; the "cancer" of whose existence he had been just as certain had stopped gnawing away at the vitals of his body and mind. Yet, he had told me over and over again that I was a slave driver and a torturer.

How can an analyst who seems so benign to one patient appear so malignant to the next one entering his office? And how can he answer as well to the equally contradictory terms in which other patients refer to him?

There is a simple explanation for this apparent paradox. It reassures me that I am not really the tormentor that Hector accuses me of being; but it also robs me of the exaggerated sense of self-esteem which Rose inspires. Neither of them, I remind myself, is talking about me. I am forced to admit that the person I really am is of little significance to any of my patients. They do not respond realistically to my presence and to the professional nature of our relationship, once this gets under way, until it is about to terminate.

A patient's freedom to talk about everything that occurs to him and my way of functioning as the instrument of his treatment dramatically intensify the characteristic strivings of his mind to produce an identity between past and present situations in his life. In the course of producing that identity, he involuntarily comes to regard me as he regarded the significant figures of his childhood; and he transfers to me feelings and attitudes which were patterned in his early relationships. I represent the images which exist in his mind, and I reawaken the emotions which surround these mental images.

Man's inborn capacity to associate feelings developed for one person with another person was one of Freud's most important discoveries. He called it *transference*.

The attitudes of Rose and Hector indicate how transference operates in individual analytic treatment. Rose was not exposed to an inordinate amount of frustration during the first few years of her life. Her relations with both parents were relaxed and gratifying to her—too much so, in some respects. Having been permitted to "blow off steam" in their presence, she did so with the utmost spontaneity during her sessions whenever the recall of some distasteful experience aroused her anger. After one of her brief explosive outbursts, she felt free to enjoy the rest of the session. For Hector, on the other hand, emotional release was an ordeal because his parents had not conditioned him to give vent to his feelings. During early and prolonged bouts with frustration, he had developed the unhealthy habit of "stewing in his own juice." As memories of these situations were kindled by my frustrating attitude [1] in the sessions, the negative feelings generated by the childhood experiences were reawakened and directed to me.

Detected or undetected, transference operates to some extent in all human relations, but the analytic psychotherapist fosters it and makes tactical use of it, because it eases the process of uncovering and coming to grips with deep-rooted conflicts. The spontaneous reactivation of unhealthy emotional attitudes during analysis usually leads

[1] In other words, my withholding of gratification. When used in reference to the treatment process, *frustration* denotes delayed gratification. The objective of the analyst is not to disappoint or defeat but to increase the patient's capacity to postpone gratification of his wishes.

to the actual or symbolic recall of long-forgotten events or relationships which were significantly linked with these attitudes.

Since the mind has ways of blotting painful realities out of consciousness, the original history of these conflicts has usually gone "out of print." By reawakening feelings and kindling memories, transference helps to revive these disturbances so that they may be analyzed and resolved in the treatment relationship. In this "new edition" of the conflict, as Freud called it, the analyst emerges as the central protagonist, appearing first in the guise of one or more persons in the patient's original history. Later on, he serves as their deconditioning agent, helping the patient to modify troublesome feelings and develop new ones which will facilitate more desirable patterns of behavior.

This dual role transforms the analyst into a phantom figure, chameleonic and intangible. To maintain the transference, he submerges himself in whatever parts fall to him in the re-enactment of the life drama. Working consistently to secure the flow of feelings toward himself and to respond to the inner needs of his patient, the analyst rarely emerges as a totally distinct personality in his own right.

Hopefully, the compulsive repetition of the emotional disorder in the transference relationship will bring it to an end, and lead to lasting changes for the better in the patient's mental life. As he gradually becomes better adjusted to reality, his impressions of the analyst become less and less distorted. The phantom figure of the transference slowly recedes into the background, and the analyst stands revealed in his true identity.

When this treatment process is carried on in the group setting, many changes take place. One of the more obvious ones is in the form and spirit of the communications. In individual treatment the personal history flows along as in autobiographical narrative. Feelings bound up in the patient's images of childhood figures are transferred to the analyst in a sustained and consistent way. Generally he does not fit himself into more than one image at a time, since the same emotional tone is held throughout a treatment session. The members of a therapy group relive their experiences more dynamically, through their spontaneous interchanges as well as through their memories. They can strike many different feeling tones during a session, covering the whole scale of human emotions in their fantasies. Hence, the group presentation of emotional conflicts is close to drama.

Another striking change is in the functioning of the phantom figure. When I started to carry on this role in the face-to-face group encounter, after serving for years as a dimly seen and little heard presence behind the analytic couch, I felt as if I were emerging from a shady nook into the midday sun. The greater abundance of sensory clues to my real identity as well as the presence of many additional stimuli have a profound effect on transference.

The more rounded and lifelike impressions which patients get of me encourage speculation about my thoughts and feelings, and also about my personal life, much earlier than in individual therapy. On the other hand, their impressions and also their fantasies about me are less sustained and less emotionally charged. The feelings which they develop for each other mitigate the effects of their feelings for me.

Indeed, transference does not operate independently of the law of supply and demand. The group setting shatters the monopoly which the therapist enjoys in the individual relationship as the only object available for the investment of mental energy, and thrusts him into a highly competitive situation. It is a buyer's market which offers a wealth of offerings—emotional bonds with other patients as well as with the group leader. For this reason, "impulse buying" is rather common. As patients shop around among the more obscure offerings, even the inflection of a voice or an almost imperceptible mannerism can touch off a startling emotional reaction. One unconscious involvement of this sort between a man and woman produced so many verbal explosions in the early sessions that one of their co-members asked them: "Is this a love duet or a war?"

Naturally, the phantom figure enjoys a favored position on the transference market. Group members characteristically take the attitude that an emotional investment in their therapist is the most profitable they can make. The respected authority, the professional healer, they customarily relate to him as to their parents.

Rather typically, a man and a woman in one group transferred to me their feelings for their own father, while I kindled memories of both parents in another group member. To a fourth, I represented the kind of person he had wanted his own mother to be; the fifth identified me with the "ideal" father of his fantasies. Jim, the sixth member of the group, reacted realistically at all times to my presence, but became emotionally involved early in treatment with a woman in his group who reminded him of his mother, and with a man who kindled memories of Jim's boyhood quarrels with his younger brother. Jim's disclosures and his hostility induced a violent counterreaction in his group "brother" and stimulated him to recall similar childhood scraps with his own brother. The two adult strangers tangled together like angry siblings in the same household.

Members of a group gradually become aware that they must go on talking about themselves throughout treatment but that the therapist does not intend to give them any information about himself. His impersonal attitude tends to reawaken the feelings which they developed early in life in frustrating situations. When, on the other hand, he "feeds" them gratifying words or attitudes, they frequently respond as they did when their infantile cravings were satisfied. Hence, the phantom figure is both the "good parent" and the "bad parent."

Accordingly, identical impressions of the therapist as an omnipotent parental figure will cause one group member to regard him as a prince of heaven, while another patient takes him to be the devil's own helper. The phantom figure who seems to have a wonderful understanding of one patient's problems can appear to another a few minutes later as an evil genius controlling everything going on in the group. In one session, a woman described me as a master of painless healing, and a man shouted at me in fury: "You should have worked for the Inquisition."

These antithetical attitudes are obscured by numerous fleeting images in the course of a session. I have been accused of egging on one patient to attack another and of sabotaging a third member's treatment, only to be told a few minutes later that I have been acting bored and disgusted and had better stop daydreaming. When a young woman's sexual problems were under scrutiny in a mixed group, one of her male treatment mates jealously envisioned me as a lady-killer. The spotlight then focused for some time on a young man and I touched off homosexual fantasies. As I work to get infantile cravings, grotesque images, and forgotten fears put into words during a group session, I play roles in many unfinished family dramas.

It is not easy to keep track of all the roles I am assigned, since transference reactions in the group are apt to be evanescent. Some of the patients assign me many different roles in the course of treatment. Those who relate to me throughout as to their father or mother may transfer their feelings for the other parent to the group as a whole or distribute them among their co-members. A group member's feelings for a parent at one stage of childhood may be transferred to the image of the therapist, while those formed earlier or later in life for that parent are reawakened by a co-member.

More consistently, patients relate to each other as they once related to sisters, brothers, and other relatives. Because of the similarity of the group configuration to that of the family, the atmosphere is often charged with "reincarnations" of siblings, cousins, and even of aunts, uncles, and grandparents.

"You're out to torture me just like my sister," one woman in a group told another. A man was told that he sounded just like the brother of another member. The speaker added: "I could never understand him either." When the origin of the feelings transferred is recognized and verbalized, the first step has been taken in the resolution of the transference reaction. Though the feeling persists, the speaker is able to control it to some extent. After that, he begins to behave more realistically.

When group members re-experience past situations in treatment, they usually reactivate their own patterns of behavior as children. In some instances a patient will, however, behave like the person toward whom his feelings were originally directed. After ridiculing another woman in her group for several sessions, Jane realized that she was identifying with her mother, who had frequently taunted Jane about her gauche conduct at family parties. In other group situations, Jane identified with herself as a child. She inexplicably shouted at a man in her group who reminded her of her father. Later on, the mystery was cleared up by her passing reference to the fact that her father was hard of hearing.

It is important for group members to develop intense feelings during the treatment sessions and to talk about them. Their reactions to me and to each other help me uncover the essential facts about their functioning, which eventually have to be conveyed to them in a therapeutic way. Nevertheless, the study of transference reactions is a subordinate aspect of the treatment process. Throughout the sessions, I am primarily concerned with another phenomenon.

"What has to happen here?" asked one woman, mystified at the absence of any formal instructions during her first session. "What is our purpose?"

"We have our own reasons for being here," another member answered. "I don't think the group has a purpose. Maybe it will develop one."

Each of them does come with a conscious purpose in mind. He also has an unconscious purpose, but this is unknown to him at the beginning. Usually many hours pass before he fully realizes that the treatment experience is designed primarily to help him understand his emotional problems and, if he so chooses, to help him resolve them. The choice is always his to make.

I gradually educate the group member to the idea that his main responsibility is to communicate his past experiences, his feelings, thoughts, and memories, and to help his co-members do the same. Words are the only currency authorized for this transaction, I indicate—words spoken spontaneously and with feeling.

"Love and hate, and say so," I tell my patients.

When a group functions in this way, something besides transference is bound to occur. The other striking phenomenon, which Freud also discovered, is *resistance*. Each patient develops unconscious resistances to what he has consciously agreed to do. However eager he is to get over his problems and however much time and money he spends to do so, he circumvents treatment in various ways. Precisely how he goes about it depends on his personality structure; his resistances reflect the defenses he developed in adjusting himself to family living as a young child.

For example, although the group member knows that he is permitted, and expected, to talk freely about himself, he tends to censor his own disclosures on subjects which would be taboo in ordinary social groups, such as perverse sex practices, personal weaknesses, and violent hatreds. Embarrassment, shame, fear, and guilt dam up some facts about himself. He shuts off his feelings at times. He may also resist more crassly, for instance by coming late to sessions or not at all. Resistance is basically similar in individual and group treatment, but much more difficult to keep track of and to understand in the group. In addition to his resistances to the group therapist's presence and frustrating behavior, each member manifests—and generates—other resistant behavior in his co-members.

The development of resistance is inevitable. Patients are incapable of engaging consistently in the kind of communications demanded of them at the beginning of treatment until they have successfully completed it. The early psychoanalysts generally discouraged resistant behavior; they tried to overcome it as quickly as possible through their interpretations, because it prevented the patient from functioning as an emotionally mature and well-adjusted person.

A significant change has taken place in the handling of resistances with the increasing recognition that they have a distinct social and personal value. Many patients need to resist talking about themselves in order to maintain their equilibrium in the group. Moreover, the patterns of resistant behavior they engage in give us many clues to their problems, just as pain and fever alert us to the ills of the body. Consequently, many analytic therapists today regard resistances as disguised or primitive forms of communication rather than as obstacles to recovery.

That is my approach. I often help group members to resist talking about themselves in order to find out why and how they permit themselves to be swerved from their task. I join them in their defenses against uncovering their basic needs and expose them to dosages of frustration so that they will refeel and manifest these needs in their treatment sessions. They are then helped to recognize and taught how to meet these needs. The more self-understanding, self-command, and tolerance to frustration they acquire in the process, the more successful I have been in treating them.

Since there is never any pushing for results, this method of functioning appears totally inefficient to anyone who is not aware of the total treatment plan. Group members often wonder: What is going on here? They call attention to the non-participation of a co-member, and I support him in his silence while trying to find out the reason for it. One woman who found it difficult to preserve her emotional integrity during her first few group sessions realized that the other patients wanted her to talk; she attempted to explain her silence. I praised her for making the attempt; then, to help her continue to resist talking, I assured her that her embarrassment about revealing intimate details of her life was natural. Resistant behavior often meets with understanding and mild commendation while its causes are being investigated.

The improvement or correction of behavior is not my primary concern. I address myself directly to the emotional tendencies which have led to the formation of undesirable patterns of behavior and hampered the development of more desirable ones. When the impediments to good functioning are cleared away, the group member is helped to trace the origins of his troublesome behavior and become capable of conducting himself the way he wishes.

The individual problems, which show up dramatically in the interchanges, are approached as factors which prevent good group functioning. Learning to work well together is part of the treatment process.

The feelings which each patient transfers to me and to his co-members are also raw material for analysis. However, these feelings are quietly studied and allowed to develop until they interfere with self-revelation. Then they are dealt with in the same way as other resistances. I therefore conceive of the whole treatment process as one of helping group members resolve all of the obstacles to free communication.

Group members assist me a great deal in analyzing as well as catalyzing feelings. The first phase of group treatment is much easier than that of individual treatment because they are quick to point out inappropriate attitudes and forms of resistant behavior which they themselves don't engage in. Consequently, a rapid alleviation of their symptoms usually takes place during the first four or five months. As they slowly acquire the ability to investigate each other's problems without developing undesirable states of irritation or tension, I follow the flow of the communications but intervene only rarely. Later on my task is much harder, especially in the final phase of treatment, when the patients are apt to confront me with common attitudes and to defy me as a unit. They are more difficult to handle then than when they individually opposed the analytic process. I have less assistance from them, and must rely solely on my own resources to resolve the group problem which they present.

My general policy in both individual and group treatment is to focus first on clearing away the obstacles to the verbal discharge of feelings of hostility, so that patients will develop the ability to get anger out of their systems. Later on, barriers to the verbal expression of affection receive high priority.

This policy developed out of my experience in the individual treatment of cases of severe emotional disorders. As I studied the various ways the patients checked, concealed, or buried their feelings as they talked about themselves, I got the impression that they had been exposed to excessive frustration during their formative years, and often later as well. Their needs may have been exceptional, or within normal limits but difficult for their parents to understand. The patients also appeared to have responded to undue frustration by developing patterns of bottling up resentment and rage—as children are often taught to do by the family and society—until these feelings became psychologically indigestible. I observed, too, that the patients thirsted intensely for love but were incapable of giving or receiving it until they had learned how to release in language the pent-up hostility which made them feel that they were split apart, or disintegrating.

Although problems of this sort do not emerge in every case, getting patients to feel free to hate me has generally

proved to be more important than getting them to feel free
to love me. In group treatment, moreover, they are more
capable of serving as "loving healers" to each other after
they have discharged much of their hostility to the phantom
figure.

I concentrate as much as possible on the group and sub-
group phenomena, making many interpretations of the
patterns of resistant behavior which all or most of the
members engage in. As much as possible, too, I interpret
other patterns of behavior in relation to what is going on
in the group as a whole. "All of you are hating each other
and trying to hide it," I told one group repeatedly during
its early sessions. When its members became irritated but
voiced no objection to the tendency of one woman to grab
the center of the stage, I brought the situation to their
attention by asking: "Why are all of you so willing to let
Hannah do all the talking, and why is she so willing to
oblige you?"

As one deals with the various factors which impede free
communication without exposing group members to undue
pressure to talk about themselves, a spontaneous drift toward emotional evolution takes place. It was this general
approach through which the man whose story follows
achieved basic changes in his personality under the influence
of analytic group process and transference.

He was an actor whose name was rather well known on
Broadway. I shall refer to him as Bart. He requested individual psychotherapy and indicated a strong need for it
when he entered treatment at the age of thirty-three. He
complained especially of his inability to settle down as a
"normal simple male."

Bart's amazingly detached way of functioning in his
individual sessions made it difficult for us to develop an

effective working relationship and for me to give him the emotional experience which he needed. Though he objectively reviewed the tragic events of his childhood, their impact upon him seemed to be beyond recall. His mother had killed herself when he was three. Four years later, an automobile accident had taken his twelve-year-old sister out of his life just as suddenly. As a child, he had hardly known his father, a construction engineer whose work kept him abroad and on the move most of the time. Over the years since his wife's death, the father had maintained clandestine relations with women wherever his duties took him.

Bart's love life was not unlike his father's. With a hail and a farewell, he turned his feelings on and off for attractive young women of the theater or café society. The more unattainable they appeared to be, the more ardently he pursued them; but all zest went out of the chase after the prize allowed herself to be captured. For the man who was suddenly separated from his mother very early in life, it is usually the elusive and unknown woman who has the greatest charm. Bart's intense nostalgia for new faces and experiences seemed to be connected with his yearning for the mother he had never really known.

He spoke of himself as the gay deceiver who had lost his gaiety. He recognized that the role kindled less and less excitement in him, but he seemed unable to shed it. Women always asked more than he could give, he maintained. That was why marriage did not appeal to him, even though he had expected to settle down in middle age with a family.

"My father will leave behind him only me, this mixed-up guy," he told me, "but it looks as if I will do worse. My thirties are going fast, and here I am still chasing rainbows in my make-believe world. I haven't met any woman I'd spend the rest of my life with and make the mother of my children."

The actor's mildly positive transference to me produced few memories of the vital emotional experiences of his childhood. It was hard for him to respond feelingly to our relationship and, when he did, to become aware of his feelings. All of his emotionality seemed to be reserved for the theater.

Bart's preoccupation with figuring out my responses to his problems helped to explain why our partnership did not mobilize his feelings sufficiently. He seemed to feel that he was sitting in my chair instead of lying on the couch. He had developed a tendency of aping whomever he was with to fence himself off from his own painful feelings; those of other people gave him more security. I got the impression that, in a group, his treatment might actually be facilitated by this tendency. He would be likely to step out of my shoes and into the shoes of other patients; their emotionality might make him more aware of his own painful feelings.

Bart agreed with me that it might be a good idea for him to meet with other patients. In the hope that they would help him discover his own identity, we decided to go on with his treatment in a group. I placed him in a new one with three other men and four women.[2] They met with me in my office one afternoon a week.

Initially, Bart functioned in the group much as he had when alone with me. He really didn't want to talk about himself. Since all he had was a "head" problem, he saw no need to put his impulses into words, words, words. There

[2] Since the separation of one life strand from the others in a group's closely woven fabric creates a badly focused group picture, it should be borne in mind that the problems of these seven other patients were being dealt with at the same time.

was only one thing wrong with him: He was too sane to be happy. Besides, the group was too immature to trust with the story of his life.

"I have a better plan," he told his co-members. "I'm going to let you work on me."

Work on him they did, but not as Bart had expected. The women irritated him by what they said, and even more by the way they said it. Why couldn't they talk about themselves without getting excited? Was it absolutely necessary, he asked them, to shriek, gesticulate, and even to weep on occasion? His air of superiority as he calmly chided them for inappropriate behavior was not easy for them to stomach.

Nor was the brutal objectivity of his criticism of them acceptable, as a rule, though from time to time one of the women recognized that he was trying to be helpful. For example, Martha, an emotionally withdrawn spinster in her late forties, thanked him for saying that her ego was as brittle as an eggshell; and Stella, a vivacious divorcée in her mid-thirties, perked up when the actor described her in such terms as flippant, insecure, and irresponsible. But Shirley and Ann took violent exception to many of Bart's remarks about them. Strong-willed and disputatious Shirley, who was thirty-two, was called a murderess because of her tendency to interrupt the others to give her own version of what they were saying. Ann, at twenty-eight the group "baby," was coldly rebuked for the opposite reason: She longed to create life. When she talked repetitiously about her desire to get married and have a child, he told her: "I won't make it and neither will you."

The angry reactions to what he regarded as constructive criticism began to creep under Bart's skin after a few sessions. Before he realized it, he, too, was speaking up in angry tones. The fact that he was becoming emotionally involved in the group give-and-take animated and agitated him.

"Something I didn't expect is happening to me here," Bart said during the fifth session. "Just listening to you speak makes me feel naked. I'm beginning to feel like a patient."

"Then name one of your problems," Martha gently taunted him.

"Yes, Bart, it's about time that you did," said Stella. "For someone who feels like a patient, you act surprisingly like an assistant therapist. Are you getting a share of our fees?"

Another month went by before Bart yielded to the mounting pressure to talk about himself. Then he launched into his first significant disclosure with the statement that he was "boiling mad." Since the group had made him feel this way, it would have to help him make an important decision.

He talked at length about an actress named Pearl. She was young and beautiful. She had been stranded between plays the previous summer when Bart, to help her out, gave her the use of his apartment while he was abroad visiting his father. Finding her still unemployed on his return, he didn't have the heart to turn her out. "But there was a clear understanding that this arrangement would end as soon as she got another part," he went on, "so she stepped into our affair with her eyes open. Besides, she'd had one unfortunate marriage and didn't want another one. That, at least, is what she said six months ago."

But the situation had changed since then. Pearl was after him to marry her; she said she was in love with him. Did he love her? Bart wasn't sure. He didn't expect to meet up with a more attractive woman, but he wasn't sure he wanted her around any more and here she was trying to tie him up for life. A woman who would rush him into marriage just because he had done so much for her out of the goodness of his heart didn't strike him as very levelheaded. In fact, she seemed definitely disturbed at times, and she triggered him off the wrong way when he felt tender. She didn't understand him, and this made her seem really hateful.

The first to respond was Robert, a forty-five-year-old business executive whose anxieties centered about his two divorced wives and three children. To convey his dim view of such goings-on, he asked: "What do you expect us to do about this?"

"Help me get off the rack," Bart pleaded. "I wish I knew why I'm having so much trouble ending this affair. Probably it's the idea of making a complete break that is so paralyzing. Age is beginning to tell against me. In my twenties, every girl I knew ran after me; but they don't eye me and crowd around now the way they did then. If I don't marry Pearl, I may never get married. But what kind of a wife would she be? When I try to explain something to her very calmly, she flies off the handle. That gets me started, and there we are in the midst of another brawl."

"If you talk to her the way you do here, that's easy to understand," Martha told him. "Probably you call her a confessed psychotic or some of the other horrible things you've called us."

"I've told her she's driving me out of my mind, but that's the simple truth," Bart replied. "I'm not mean or malicious; I just try to show her how she really is. But she can't take it. That rubs me the wrong way, just as you women do here. Under the skin, there is something about each one of you that reminds me of Pearl."

Henry thought it would be hard for her not to react

to Bart's general hostility to women. An engineer who worried about his own unpopularity with them, Henry himself was shocked by Bart's attitude.

"I don't think you only hate her," said Shirley. "If there wasn't something else between you two, you wouldn't be in this stew. Anyway, don't you think you could learn to love her?"

"Whatever you decide, you're in for trouble," Robert asserted. "You'd be miserable if you married her. She sounds as if she'd make a terrible wife and ruin your children. But if you break off with her, you'll go through the same thing with the next woman—if you find one who wants you."

That was my cue. "Robert is absolutely right, Bart," I told him, "but there's a simple way out of this mess. Forget Pearl and think about marrying one of the women in this group. You'd be sure to have a nice understanding wife. You're developing warm feelings for all of them. In no time you'll be falling in love with someone here. Otherwise, if you don't want Pearl to lose her appeal for you, you'd better marry her quickly."

"That's to keep you from making an unwise decision— he knows you'll do the opposite," said Max, who was trying to read my mind. A lawyer, and at thirty-nine still a bachelor, he found it easier to talk about mental telepathy than about his personality and career problems.

"That's not so," I contradicted Max. "All I'm saying is that you'll fall in love with a stranger. You'll find at least one woman here whom you'll love."

"No woman is lovable once you get to know her," Bart replied gloomily.

"But you'll never get to know these women," I told him. "You can't date them and you can't pop into bed with them. You'll see them just once a week here in this office. That's just long enough for you to develop intense feelings for them. You won't have to look for any other woman, so your problem will be solved."

"Too bad that Pearl isn't a member of the group," Henry quipped.

"I don't want her here," Shirley snapped at him. "She can go to a marriage counselor."

"I second that," said Ann. She was also encouraged by my prediction. "There's more than enough competition here now."

Martha, outclassed in looks and youthfulness, liked to demonstrate that she was an understanding person. "Bart says that the women here remind him of Pearl," she stated, "but he hasn't said anything about Pearl reminding him of someone. His mother, perhaps?"

"I didn't know my mother," he replied. "She died when I was only three. Killed herself, in a fit of depression. My father was off in the Philippines on a construction project. They quarreled when he was home, and she refused to jump around the world from job to job with him. He returned home one day to find her dead."

"And I'm dead, too, according to you." Stella sounded triumphant as she reminded Bart of something he had told her. "It's your notion that women are crazy or they're dead. At least, that's the way you treat us here. Is that wishful thinking?"

"What a female!" Bart exclaimed. "She accuses me of death wishes for her because I've tried to help her. And when I ask for help, she insists on goading me. That's a downright mean woman for you."

"Thanks for saying that. Thanks very much." Stella always seemed pleased to be the center of attraction. "All

my life I've been waiting for someone to call me mean;
everyone says I'm too kind. Being a goody-goody is not
my idea of life. I want to be a real human being with plenty
of salt and plenty of pepper."

"So that's why you've been hounding me from the start,"
Bart remarked. "I thought something was going on here.
It's about time you cut it out."

Max's impression that I functioned in that session to
prevent Bart from making an unwise decision was mislead-
ing. I was not trying to help him make up his mind about
Pearl. I don't try to control the conduct of patients; dic-
tating, persuading, or even suggesting what they should do
is contrary to analytic process. As a matter of fact, I am
not primarily concerned with the current situation to
which I appear to be responding—in this case, Bart's conflict about the marriage which he consciously thought he
wanted and the loveless and irresponsible existence which
he had been conditioned to live. What is going on in the
group at the moment is always the important factor. I so
couch my interventions that they appear to be directed to
the problem which is being consciously presented. I deal
with this as literally and inoffensively as possible because
this permits me to work on the unconscious problem.

I speak when I want to make an emotional impact on a
patient, mobilize feelings he is unaware of, or help him to
put them into words. Some of these interventions are
designed primarily to alert him to the emotional realities of
a situation in a therapeutic way. Other statements are formulated to release him from the mental shackles which
interfere with his talking freely about his feelings and
thoughts.

I had both motives in mind during that session. Moreover, I was concerned with what was going on in the group

as a whole. My statements, though nominally addressed to Bart alone, also applied to the behavior of the others during the sessions. They, too, though to a lesser degree, were either unaware that they were developing feelings of love for each other or were concealing these feelings in indifference, contempt, or hatred. I wanted to stimulate them to recognize and talk about all of their feelings. In this sense, I was making a group interpretation.

As far as Bart himself was concerned, my motive was more specific. One of his conscious goals in entering treatment was to become capable of changing his way of life; he wanted to marry and settle down. In his individual sessions, he had intellectually accepted the idea that he was driven in the opposite direction by his feelings. They tied him down to the kind of life he was leading and explained his unconscious struggle against love as an insidious force that would trap him into domesticity. A woman who loved him was therefore someone to be eliminated from his mind; his own love for a woman was to be stifled or concealed with hatred. He understood that this was the emotional logic of his irrational behavior, but this understanding had not produced a change in the feelings which impelled him to behave as he did.

Bart responded to the women in the group more emotionally than he had responded to me in his individual sessions; his interchanges with them tended to mobilize feelings he was not aware of. My objective at that point was to help him get those feelings into words. The process of verbalizing them would itself lessen his tendency to act on them, but even more vital was the need to explore them from many different points of view in the sessions.

The interpretations I made focused specifically on the two contrary impulses which were so troublesome to Bart.

His impulse to lead a sensible life was threatened by his impulse to go on behaving like a jaded Don Juan. To upset the uneasy equilibrium which he had achieved between those impulses, I was striking at the barrier which kept him from talking about his impulse to continue his present irrational way of life. If this impulse could be "tamed" by a combination of verbal release and understanding, his behavior would be more amenable to the dictates of his reason.

The impact of Stella's transference reactions on Bart gave me a great deal of help in making him aware of this deeply rooted conflict. Her feelings were easy to keep track of, since they "leaked" into her gestures and behavior. In one session, for instance, instead of expressing her contempt for Max in words, she demonstrated it by putting her hands to her ears and turning her back to him when he talked. When he voiced his anger, she drew her hand across her throat instead of telling him: "I'd like to cut your throat." The acting out of feelings during the sessions or in daily life in the course of treatment interferes with talking about them, so it is generally regarded as non-co-operative behavior. This pattern of resistance is not uncommon, but Stella engaged in it with unusual vehemence. Reminders that she was "acting out" the various impulses stirring in her from moment to moment were often necessary. At times the reminders stimulated her to remember some significant event in her life.

In relating certain painful impressions of her childhood, Stella talked with contempt or indifference about her mother, sister, and brother. Her memories of her father, who died when she was eighteen years old, aroused her deepest emotions. In her transference to me at first, I detected the feelings she had developed for him. She talked about being his favorite child, and she tried to secure the same preferential position in my group "family." Her incessant demands for attention and approval, which induced resentment in her new "siblings," made it easy to see how she had conducted herself as a child within her own family circle.

After maintaining this attitude toward me rather consistently during the first two months of group activity, Stella's transference reactions to me began to fluctuate. First of all, her feelings for me as a father figure became perceptibly less intense as Bart began to reawaken certain other feelings she had developed for her father. Later on, a more decided shift in her feelings for me took place while Bert's indecision about marriage was a hotly debated issue.

As he seesawed between the alternatives of marriage or a complete break with Pearl, the actor demonstrated the tendency of group members to fluctuate sharply in their mental images of parents and other persons they talk about during the sessions. He painted highly contradictory pictures of the young actress; either she was wonderful or she was crazy. His attitudes about continuing to be a member of the group veered just as sharply during this period. At times, he would say that he had made a mistake in leaving individual treatment; at other times, he seemed equally convinced that he belonged in the group.

My interpretations continued to refer to the conflict about the outside relationship. However, I was primarily concerned with what was going on inside the group at that time. Why and how did they conceal feelings of love or the rivalry which they stimulated in each other? Why and how did they express these feelings? I focused on the answers they involuntarily gave me to questions such as these.

In one session, Bart cited an incident which proved to him that Pearl was "wacky."

"I can't imagine why you don't get rid of her," said Shirley.

"Love me instead," Stella suggested.

"Many women have wanted my love," Bart told her. "But there they are and who wants them?"

"You really are in trouble, aren't you?" she responded. "Anyway, I'd like to feel some love from you."

Stella was a woman who brimmed over with feelings and frequently surrendered to them. To find out how certain she was of herself, I once remarked that she was about as responsive as a block of ice. The absurdity of this statement was immediately recognized by the others, but it took some time for her to realize that I had actually meant the reverse.

Her responses were generally hard to anticipate. Stella was frequently invigorated by comments which would have crushed or angered many persons. She thanked Bart for saying that she impressed him as being psychologically dead; hearing it had made her "come alive again," she reported later. The substance of his remarks was relatively unimportant to her. Because of her deep craving for his attention, she responded to his objective criticisms as if they were the sentiments of a perceptive lover. I suspected that she had reacted the same way as a youngster when her father's attitude impressed her as being hostile. Perhaps any kind of attention from him made her feel vital and worthwhile.

Bart's rejecting attitude seemed to intensify her craving for his love. At the beginning of one group session, she said that she had come only to be with him. Her complete indifference to what went on during that meeting told me that my quiet and detached study of her "transference love" for Bart was no longer appropriate. The overexcitement which this love created in her was provoking her to act out her impulses more than ever. Her transference to Bart would have to be resolved because it now impeded rather than helped her talk with real feeling.

My cue to begin handling it as a resistance came during the following meeting. Stella dared Bart to take her out on a date. When he refused, she suggested that he was afraid he might get to like her if he saw her outside my office. I reminded her that this would interfere with therapy. Besides, if her love for him were mature and unselfish, she would make a real effort to understand and help him instead of trying to lure him into a love affair. The group experience was designed for the lasting emotional benefit of the whole group, not for the momentary gratification of one of its members.

A startling transformation in Stella's feelings for me took place during the next few sessions. The phantom figure which had revived her feelings for her father seemed to have been relegated to an entirely different role in her fantasies. I sensed that it had become a highly frustrating presence. I wondered if she now related to it as she had to her mother when she was unconsciously regarded as standing between Stella and her father.

This hypothesis about her negative transference to me during that phase of treatment was eventually confirmed by Stella. The picture became clear from her comment on a statement by Max that he found it very hard to say anything that afternoon. Seconding the complaint, she said that it was practically impossible for her to talk about herself in the group. "It makes me sad," Stella went on, "but what's the use of talking to my big bad mother?"

The embarrassed silences with which Bart met her professions of love were in sharp contrast with his increasingly friendly manner to the other women. I sensed that Stella's emotional involvement with him had introduced a disturbing new element in his relations with Pearl. Could she have sensed it too?

Bart's report of an ultimatum from Pearl that she would leave him if he continued to waver created a flurry of excitement. His attitude made it clear that the prospect of marrying her had become less threatening to his equilibrium than the prospect of a complete break. Did he unconsciously feel the need for some protection against another woman? He reacted angrily to each reminder of his own misgivings or of the black pictures he had painted of Pearl. After stubbornly defending her against his own accusations, he brought the excitement to a peak by announcing that they were to be married in a few days.

The group tried to talk Bart out of marrying Pearl, but he would not budge. Told by Martha that it would be a catastrophe to marry a "wacky" woman, Bart retorted: "Prove to me that she's insane. That's the only thing that will stop me from marrying her."

Since the others could not pass judgment on someone whom they had never seen, this position was unassailable.

One week later Bert calmly informed the group that the ceremony had taken place. The women, braced for the blow, made only brief comment.

"What a disaster," Ann murmured.

"For years you spited yourself by not marrying," Martha told him. "Now you spite yourself by marrying a woman you don't love."

"I've been spurned," Stella said, "but I haven't given up."

The men were more favorably disposed to the marriage.

Henry congratulated Bart and solemnly added: "We taught you here to live with society."

"It was something I had to do," he answered. "You speeded me toward it."

In more than one sense, this seemed to be true. The negatively suggestible actor had been spurred on by the intensity of the group's opposition. Besides, his own transference reactions made Bart exceptionally vulnerable to the group situation.

The women in the group, he bluntly remarked on more than one occasion, were too old or not "wild and sexy enough" for him. Besides, he consciously accepted the idea that he was not supposed to have any contact with them outside the treatment sessions. Nevertheless, the fact that they bombarded him with expressions of love and that one of them wanted to have an affair with him was dangerously exciting to a man who habitually succumbed with childish weakness to the new woman on his horizon who wanted to make love to him. The thought that he might, somewhere, be denied sexual gratification had once thrown him into a panic, Bart told the group.

When he made this significant disclosure, he was talking about his travels abroad, but unknowingly Bart was reacting to what was going on in the group. The requirement that he only talk—and talk freely in the presence of strangers—about his sexual desires made treatment a highly frustrating experience. Objective criticism and the provoking of hostility were his unconscious defenses in this situation, but these were weakened when the women came to understand them. His sensitivity to Stella's love exposed him to the danger of preferring a woman in the group whom he did not know to a girl he did know and liked well enough to consider marrying. In a veritable panic at the thought of acting again in this highly impulsive manner, Bart finally mobilized himself to marry Pearl as a protection against the other woman.

He thought that this step would demonstrate that he had mastered his irrational tendencies, but I did not agree with him. As I interpreted it, flinging himself impetuously at that juncture into a situation which he had avoided for so many years was like jumping into the fire because the frying pan was too hot to handle.

Bart eventually decided that there was a rational way out of the situation: to make a success of the marriage. It was a course that appealed to him, though it made the working out of his emotional problems more crucial than ever. The group helped him to resolve them. It did not do so, however, by advising him how to cope with the matrimonial stress and strain which he frequently reported to us during the months which followed. Quite the contrary. This information was investigated and utilized to help him understand why he felt and acted as he did in the group sessions, and to help him behave more appropriately.

The resolution of the old conflict between his emotions and his reason made Bart capable of being a good husband and father. It also gave him the freedom to embark on any other course which might seem more desirable to him. None did. The success of his marriage was assured because he found the roles of husband and father more satisfying than any other he had ever played.

To be fully understood, a group-treatment experience has to be studied in retrospect. While it is going on, session after session gives rise to countless speculations about the origin of the members' feelings for me and for each other; but I never know how close I am to the emotional core of their problems while these feelings are developing. Nor do

I want to know, for this might interfere with my spontaneity and inhibit analytic activity by making it a purely intellectual process. One sudden flash may light up the whole nuclear problem or it may have to be reconstructed from many minute elements. In either case, the truth always comes later, as a product of our work together.

It then becomes clear to me why a group member had the various feelings for me and his co-members which I sensed in a particular treatment situation. Ultimately, all of these feelings fit into his life history as neatly as the separate pieces of a picture fit into a child's puzzle. When this history is fully assembled, it is easy to comprehend why each feeling developed and how it influenced his behavior.

The patient who successfully completes treatment can generally assemble his own emotional history in the same way. He can tell the group what feelings were reawakened in him at one stage of treatment or another and to whom they were transferred. Often, he will be able to recall what it was about me or his co-patients which reminded him of some member of his own family or revived memories of significant events in his life. Bart eventually recognized, for example, that Stella symbolized for him the women from whom he had turned during his compulsive search for the new face and the fresh experience. Stella recognized the difference in the feelings which Bart and I had reawakened in her as father figures. I fitted her image of her father when she was three years old. The more erotic feelings which Bart aroused in her during many sessions matched the impressions which she had of her father seven or eight years later.

The analysis of her transference to Bart started, as I have already indicated, when it began to prevent her from talking about herself. In the course of this analysis, which proceeded in snatches during many sessions, we first investigated what it was about Bart which reminded Stella of her father. Memories of childhood situations in which he had censured her for misbehavior without betraying any emotion were reawakened by Bart's objective criticism of her during the group sessions. She had been sexually stimulated as a child by her father's critical but attentive attitude. Having regarded it as an expression of his love, she tended to respond similarly to Bart's bluntly impersonal criticism.

The differences between Stella's mental images of her father and Bart were also explored. Through this analysis, supplemented by Bart's own disclosures about himself, she gradually became aware of him as a real person. In the process, some illusions were shattered; she discovered that he was not the lover she had imagined him to be. Her attitude became more friendly and realistic, but her fantasies about him ended. As they became genuinely interested in understanding and helping each other, their interaction in the group mobilized new feelings in both of them.

When a group member is able to explain the salient facts about his own emotional development, to trace it chronologically and discuss it intelligently in the group from different perspectives, that indicates to me that he has a good understanding of himself. Explanations which are spontaneous and create significant changes in his behavior demonstrate that the adverse effects of his emotional disorder have been corrected. Feelings appropriate to all sorts of situations and human relationships have been fused into his personality in the crucible of transference.

[4]

◆◇◆◇◆◇◆◇◆◇◆◇◆

Themes with Variations

YEARS OF RESEARCH in psychoanalysis and my own psycho-analysis have sharpened my awareness of the vast amount of information which people give about themselves without intending, and sometimes without knowing that they do so. Beyond the literal meaning of their words, countless aspects of their inner life experiences can be discerned by the ana-lytically trained listener.

Many facts come to light in this way which the speakers themselves are not consciously aware of, or would not willingly divulge. Nevertheless, they can no more prevent this personal history from emerging than an animal can move through sand without depositing clues to its identity. Much as the naturalist determines the size, method of loco-motion, species, and even the physical condition of the creature by examining its footprints, I learn a great deal about my patients by studying their random behavior. Everything they do or don't do during their sessions tells me something about them.

These involuntary communications were identified in the

last chapter as resistance patterns. It was pointed out that
these are not as pure analytic ore as conscious co-operative
communications; nevertheless, they often shed light on conflicts which a patient is not consciously aware of or cannot
express in words. That is why everything he says and does
is sifted through for clues to the unconscious struggles
which have to be recognized and understood before the
desired changes can be effected.

I learn something about these troublesome inner forces
from his defensive statements. These are the words with
which he covers up his true feelings. His gestures, tone of
voice, and other "body language" are also studied, along
with his aimless actions. However, the involuntary communications which are most significant for my purpose are
not perceived through my sensory apparatus. They are the
emotions—the stored patterns of behavior—and the un-
controlled urges and impulses which are so crucial for human behavior. In the course of analytic treatment, these
vital statistics of psychic functioning are converted into
conscious, rational, and emotionally significant communications.

The group setting stimulates these involuntary messages
because they are mobilized by frustration. When the basic
urges which move the members of a therapy group are frustrated, they naturally create more intense emotional currents than those present in the two-party relationship. Besides, a person treated individually is not subjected to certain
types of frustration which are inevitable in the group
situation.

The most obvious of these is the sharing of time and
attention with other patients. The privilege of talking has
to be paid for with courteous listening. This does not mean
that the group member who is talking at any moment is

being gratified and that his co-members are being frustrated. At times, being silent is very satisfying, or it is frustrating in certain respects and satisfying in others. Varying degrees of frustration and gratification are present, and the situation is structured to keep them in healthy balance. This can get to be as complicated as it sounds.

"I am stimulated by the fact that I am not ashamed to be quiet," one man explained when questioned about his silence.

The roar of laughter which followed reflected the novelty of the idea, and also the impression of his co-patients that the speaker had found a humorous way of saying that he really did not want to talk. Actually, though, I recognized that this was the opposite of the truth. He wanted to talk very much, but he was a timid soul who had convinced himself that he was unworthy of attention. Without knowing it, he was always working to get the group to eliminate him, as he had eliminated himself. An implied meaning of his statement was that his colleagues should be ashamed of themselves for talking so much, but he really envied them for being able to do it.

On the other hand, talking about oneself without any reservations is not always easy, especially when a group is just beginning to function. It takes time to break the shackles of life training and social conventions. After the attitude that it is unbecoming to strip before strangers has been trained into a person, he has trouble exposing his psychological nakedness. Not to bare himself means a waste of time and money, but to do so too quickly may be damaging.

One way out of this dilemma is to go through the motions of self-revelation while backing away from embarrassing topics and keeping feelings under control. That is why members often start out with methodical, labored statements on subjects in which they have no real stake or are

not ready to talk about spontaneously. Some prepare mono-
logues in advance or come in with envelopes stuffed with
notes on their dreams. This is the kind of defiance through
compliance for which the good soldier Schweik is cele-
brated in fiction. At times, a new group seems full of soldier
Schweiks.

As group members resist meaningful communication,
their behavior reflects the patterns of adjustment which
they developed early in life. By studying their characteristic
reactions to frustration, I come to recognize how they were
trained to behave by their parents. I subject them to all sorts
of psychological stresses to find out how much frustration
they can stand and what kinds of behavior are easiest for
them to engage in. As they relive their infantile training
experiences in their transferences to me and to each other,
I get flashbacks of significant experiences which seem to be
linked with their emotional problems.

The spontaneous emotional exchanges in the group also
have an important communication value. I can learn a great
deal from the way a patient behaves toward other patients,
whereas when he is alone with me all I have to go by is the
way he relates to me. Instead of this single response, there
is multiple interaction evoking a wide range of responses.
The presence of several persons listening to a speaker stimulates a variety of mild or intense reactions. By comparing the
attitudes of the silent members, I can usually sense the feelings which the speaker or the subject under discussion stirs
in each of them.

When a person refuses to talk about himself with real
feeling, I pay particular attention to these spontaneous reactions. Often they are the key to some significant life
experience which has not been divulged.

This happened in the case of a woman who spent her

first four months in group therapy working against herself. Her feeling that she was too superior to be helped by anyone but myself made her a standout during that period.

Clara's behavior during the first session marked her as a consistent objector. She lost no time objecting to the practical arrangements. The hour was late and her chair was uncomfortable. Besides, I wasn't talking enough. A few sessions later, she talked about her childhood in the deliberate and impersonal manner of a schoolgirl presenting a composition in class.

The response to this approach was not encouraging, and this seemed to reinforce her original attitude of contempt for her colleagues. Besides refusing to talk with real feeling about herself, Clara made fun of the two other women in the group when they spoke with earnest simplicity about themselves. They reminded her of a character in a soap opera, she said, or of the ingénue in a high school play. While she mowed down the women with such comments, Clara's attitude toward the three men was more friendly. She chatted with them at times as if they were attending a dinner party.

She often demonstrated the difficulties in getting along with people which had brought her into treatment. The wife of a college professor and the mother of twins, then ten years old, Clara gave me the impression that these "people" might include her husband. I don't recall when or why I began suspecting this. It may have been because she never mentioned him except to say that he was "sweet."

In marked contrast to her reactions to her co-patients was her attitude to me. She clung to every word I said, and often complained that I neglected her. Someone pointed out to her that she was bored with everything except what "the boss" had to say. Members of a therapy group usually start out with this attitude, but in the normal sequence of events their conspicuous deference to the group leader wears off and they become more interested in each other's company.

Clara's attitude confronted me with the same kind of emergency that parents face when the life of one of their children is in danger. Just as the parents concentrate on saving the child, I concentrated on preventing Clara from eliminating herself from the group. I often apply this principle of family living when a group member appears to be on the verge of psychologically killing himself off or is threatened with the same fate by one of his "siblings." During that period, preserving the group as a unit meant keeping Clara in it and strengthening her ties to it.

To this end, I explored every facet of her self-isolating behavior and tried to understand it. I deliberately ignored her demands for attention while investigating her reactions to each rebuff.

In individual treatment, I wouldn't have been talking to her either. She would have accused me of being unaware of her problems and indifferent to her needs. Meanwhile, I would have been trying to figure out why she had developed this attitude and how it could best be dealt with. In the one-to-one relationship, though, I would not have had the help which the group gave me during this exploratory process.

This help, though indirect, was an important source of analytic data. In addition to the extreme contrast in Clara's responses to me and to the group as a whole, her group peers were stimulating in her more exquisitely differentiated reactions. I learned more from her distinctive attitudes to the men than to the women, to both of whom she responded with about the same degree of supercilious indifference.

While reviewing Clara's behavior during that period, I

built up various working hypotheses about her conflicts. I did not know which, if any, would be correct. "Correct" in this context requires some explanation, since it can be interpreted in different ways. For some analysts, the correct hypothesis is the one which is in conformity with Freudian theory or the concepts of some other school of psychotherapy to which they happen to subscribe. That is not what I mean by the word. In my opinion, no hypothesis is correct unless it leads to constructive inner change in the patient.

It takes a long time to develop such a hypothesis, especially when a patient is as unco-operative as this woman was. It takes an even longer time to get the patient to understand it and to produce the desired change. Since Clara's case is not yet terminated, the ultimate fate of some of my speculations about her are still in doubt; but I shall indicate how one of them was confirmed.

In trying to extract inner meanings from her random behavior and other involuntary communications during the sessions, I examined these within different frames of reference. Accepted theories about the development of the personality were in one frame. In another were the fruits of my experience with other patients and what they told me about themselves. I also looked back into my own life as a child and as an adult.

Drawing at will upon theory, other life patterns, and memories, I used my impressions and other clues to devise the kind of skeletal structure of this woman's personality which would enable me to understand why she behaved as she did and why she could not have behaved otherwise. Not until the time came to share this conditional understanding with her would I know how well I had reconstructed her life. If what I told her helped her to recall the experiences

which had trained her present attitudes into her and also led
to significant changes in her behavior, I would know that
my reconstruction was correct. Certain types of feelings,
memories, and behavior would signal the therapeutic reliving of the traumatic experiences, but only a permanent
change in her behavior would prove that I had actually
solved the problem. Only time would tell.

The vigor of Clara's objections at the start suggested a
basic inability to tolerate doing what she had consciously
agreed to do in joining the group. I wondered what early
experience was reflected in this conflict between her will
and her emotions. Could there have been some difficulty
about her presence in the family? Was she perhaps an unwanted child or, at least, an unwanted daughter? She seemed
to be communicating some attitude of unconscious rejection
which she had experienced in her infancy.

From the way she related to the other two women in the
group, I gained the impression that her mother's attitude to
her had been experienced by Clara as hostile and superior,
and that she was identifying with this attitude in her reactions to them. All I could be certain of at this point was that
she had experienced this same attitude early in her life from
someone close to her; or perhaps it had been her own attitude to someone else in her family. I would have to keep on
re-evaluating an impression like this until I was satisfied that
it was substantiated by the weight of the evidence.

Clara's distinctive ways of relating to the men gave rise
to other speculations. Bob, a phlegmatic businessman in
his forties, impressed her as being sweet-natured; she
mentioned casually during one session that he reminded her
of her husband. The witty remarks of Al, an advertising
man in his late thirties, amused her. Some of them were
rather critical, but they did not make her uncomfortable

because they were not barbed with real feeling. She responded indifferently at first to Fred, a thirty-five-year-old engineer who was usually too submerged in his feelings of worthlessness to pay much attention to what went on in the sessions.

A sudden change in Clara's attitude to Fred gave me an important clue to her mental state. Early in one session, I expressed the opinion that the group members were not making a real effort to help each other. My statement may have stimulated them to inquire into Clara's defensive reference to a dispute in which she was embroiled with a neighbor. Fred especially became interested in Clara's assertion that the neighbor was wholly to blame for the quarrel, and asked questions that were spiked with criticism. Clara did not hide her irritation. She accused him of piecing together bits of information she had given him into a distorted bill of particulars. With biting emphasis, she added that it was a "big trauma" to know him.

Fred exploded. "Clara is a real bitch. And I'm going to treat her as one from now on."

"That's the most honest thing you ever said," I told him.

My choice at that moment was between defending Clara and praising Fred. To do the former when I was not sure it would be therapeutic for her would be like muddying the water before finding out what was underneath. On the other hand, there was no doubt in my mind that praise would be desirable for Fred. Until then he had gone round and round in the groove of his own worthlessness, like a defective phonograph record, and I wanted to commend him for finally getting out of the groove. Besides, even though my remark was not directed at Clara, I had no objection to her reading other meanings into it. This might release some hostility in her, which would be desirable.

But there was no counterattack. Clara remained grimly silent. The others present did not hide their surprise. Al asked her if she couldn't think of something to say. She did not answer. Bob remarked that Clara and Fred reminded him of two infantile characters in a play he had just seen. Then the group moved on to another subject.

Clara's failure to lash back at Fred was an illuminating development. I thought about it a great deal, and compared it with her customary reactions to the other men. They gave her sweetness without feeling, and she found it acceptable. Fred had on this occasion given her feeling without sweetness and she had promptly crumpled, suggesting that it was extremely difficult for her to hold her own under attack. This, if true, would help to explain her reluctance to invest her emotions in any group encounters, since these would sooner or later expose her to intensely hostile feelings.

Although she welcomed sweetness without feeling from Al and Bob, Clara continued to seek some more significant response from me. She solicited my opinion on various subjects, and usually without success. However, I made one guarded comment which opened the door to further progress in this case.

"Why don't you cut your hair, Clara, or fix it some other way?" One of the women asked her this question in the course of a casual discussion of personal appearance and grooming. Her long blond hair was invariably drawn into a bun at the back of her head. As the speaker went on to make some suggestions for a new hairdo, Clara interrupted her to ask what I thought about her hair. I asked if she had ever tried to figure out some less severe way of fixing it. That ended the discussion.

A week later her hair was cut short and arranged with attractive simplicity. The striking change in her appearance was the subject of group comment for several sessions. She had cut her hair, she said, to please me.

Clara's irritation over my frustrating attitude became acute a few weeks later. Was I ever going to do anything to earn my money? I sat there like a mummy, she went on, and all she could think of was how bored she was with the group.

"You are the most boring person here," I told her. "You are trying to force me to give you some attention. Someone should take care of you."

Al spoke up. Didn't I realize that he was trying very hard to keep her entertained?

That was obvious, I remarked. The trouble was that there was no real bond between the two of them. "What Clara needs is real care and affection," I added. "And understanding."

Then why didn't I give her some, Clara asked. She really needed some attention. Because of me she had cut her hair and bought herself some costume jewelry. The upshot was that she was in real trouble with her husband.

"Tell your husband that you have a right to be attractive," I told her. "His objections ought to be investigated."

He thought that her new hairdo was too undignified for the wife of a professor and that the new jewelry compounded the damage. It was all junk, in his opinion, and cheapened her appearance. Still, she liked her husband very much, Clara continued. Talking about him this way made her feel very guilty.

"Tell him he'll lose you if he persists in this attitude," I interposed. "You are in conflict with your husband because you can't be yourself with him. He objects to your wearing your hair the way you want to, and he says that your new jewelry is junky. That's the symbol of your problem."

Clara defended her husband. He was very sweet, and he rarely asked her for anything.

"If you always guess what a man wants," Bob said, "he doesn't have to ask for anything."

"And that isn't all," I told her. "A man who doesn't have to ask for anything and is the sweetest guy in the world—a man who never picks a fight—that's a real killer."

I accomplished my purpose. For the first time Clara spoke to us frankly, and without trying to hide her true feelings.

In what she disclosed about her childhood at that time, there was nothing that either confirmed or disproved my speculations about her relationship with her mother. Her references to her father pointed to another sensitive area to be explored. A well-known classical scholar who had been dead several years, he had been mentioned once before in sympathetic terms; but now Clara admitted that their ties were thin and disappointing.

"My father never took the time to try to understand his children," she told the group. "We used to say he'd throw us a line of Greek if he saw us drowning."

She talked at greater length about her husband. He was an instructor at the university when she was introduced to him by her father. It became clear that she had related to the two men somewhat similarly. Her husband had failed her in one critical situation after another. But she deserved this, Clara continued, because she hadn't loved him as much as she should. On the other hand, he loved her as much as he could love anyone. She would die rather than have him know of her disappointment and anger about many things. He was much too sweet to be hurt by her. She blamed herself for being so dissatisfied and for hating him at times.

"Punishment for that kind of hatred is your own death," I told her. This was the first time she had made it possible for me to share with her my understanding of her emotional conflicts.

Her deep sigh of relief was all that I could have wished for. The sigh—like laughter, tears, feelings of being understood, fury at being discovered, and certain other eruptions of emotions—is one of the responses which is most pleasing to a psychotherapist. It told me that I was striking oil.

Clara's acceptance of my interpretation made it possible for me to tell her that, instead of having her stay home and die, we wanted to have her with us as a functioning member of the group.

Though group members rarely work as vigorously as Clara did not to give away any secrets, it is not uncommon for them to display a special hearing defect which requires equally patient handling. One woman with this difficulty was as determined to tell all about herself as Clara was to tell nothing. However, as Janet poured out thoughts and feelings so conscientiously, it soon became evident that she could not hear the simple obvious things she was saying. She was psychologically deaf to the sound of her own voice.

Shouting their own words back at them is not a therapeutic approach to persons with this difficulty. They need to hear the echo and re-echo, in other voices and contexts, of what they have been saying. Since thoughts and feelings reverberate easily in a therapy group, it is the ideal setting for this purpose. It gave Janet the kind of hearing-aid she needed.

She was a divorcée who summed up her social difficulties by saying that it was as hard for her to find the right people as to leave the wrong. She had married a man who pleased her mother; a few unhappy years later, Janet divorced him because she thought this would please her first analyst.

When the group began functioning, Janet was living with her mother and there was an intense relationship between them. How much longer they would be together was uncertain; Janet reported that she was facing a painful decision. Her mother, who had suffered for years from a degenerative disease, was becoming too mentally deteriorated to take care of herself or to be left alone in the apartment during the day. Her physician recommended that she be hospitalized as soon as possible.

Session after session, Janet brought up this problem without giving any evidence that she was moving any closer to her decision. She would insist, whenever the group tried to investigate the situation with her, that she was delaying action for only one reason: Sending her mother to an institution would be like sending her to a cemetery. How could she do that to one she loved so dearly? Much as the other members sympathized with Janet, her unadulterated repetition of this theme made them feel more and more helpless. After a while, they stopped commenting on the situation, and her reports on it were left hanging in air.

Mary, a woman in the same group who complained of social maladjustment, had rarely commented on Janet's conflict. This attracted no attention, since Mary was still having difficulty talking about herself. She had disclosed that she was a personnel director for a dress manufacturing concern. Admittedly, she was in almost daily contact with many important people in the world of fashion and had traveled widely. "But don't think there's anything glamorous about my life," Mary went on. "I'm getting no place fast."

Then Mary walked into my office one evening in a state of excitement. She was obviously under great pressure to talk.

"I suppose you all know that I've been sitting on something that I couldn't tell you before," she started off. "But my whole life has just unfolded. Now I have to talk about it."

She launched into a description of her visit over the weekend to the state hospital about two hundred and fifty miles away where her mother had spent more than thirty-five years. Since her commitment following a psychotic breakdown, she had rarely been visited by members of her family. This was Mary's first trip to the institution in twelve years. Her father, who had moved to the West Coast many years ago, was spending his vacation with her when they suddenly decided to go together. She wasn't sure what had prompted them to do so.

During their drive to the hospital, she insisted that her father tell her the true facts about her mother's breakdown. She had never known them, Mary explained, and her recollection of whatever she had been told was dim. She added: "Mostly, I guess I tried not to know more, because I was convinced I'd find out that mother's illness followed a family pattern."

Weaving her own memories into her father's story, Mary told about her father's departure from home for the Army when she was only seven. She rarely saw him during the next few years. Her mother, beset by loneliness and practical problems, drifted into an affair with a neighbor. She neglected her three children. Their father, returning home, found his wife suffering from syphilis. After that, husband and wife lived together as strangers.

About a year later, Mary's brother, three years her junior, contracted infantile paralysis and was dead within a few days. This was soon followed by her mother's mental breakdown and, when her illness was eventually diagnosed as incurable, by her commitment. At the time she had taken to her bed, Mary and her older sister were given to understand that their mother had heart disease.

Mary could recall having little feeling for her mother at the time. She had felt neglected by both parents, and the favoritism shown her brother had made her feel persecuted as well. She told the group about her mixed feelings at the time of his death and her grim satisfaction later when her mother had to leave home. Years later, Mary began to think of herself as a monster for having felt that way.

As she began to talk about the weekend meeting with her mother, one of the men interrupted her. "I'm sorry, Mary, but perhaps you'd better stop," he said. "Janet can't take this."

Janet, who had been crying, accepted the interruption as permission to sob loudly. "I can't stand it, I can't stand it," she moaned. "Don't you realize that this is happening to my mother?"

Mary glanced at me, and then resumed her account of the weekend reunion. After first mistaking her for her older sister, Mary's mother recognized her, calling her by her name and crying with joy. "She had some lucid moments," Mary continued. "She asked my father to forgive her and pray for her in church. She is still atoning. He seemed deeply moved by all this. You see, on top of the disgrace and everything else, her sickness cost him every penny he had. He lost all of his ambition, and his dignity too. He still hates her, I think, but he talks about taking her out. On the trip back, he asked me if I thought she could leave the institution."

Janet wailed: "And now I have to put my mother in one of those places. I can't stand it. Why can't you people understand that this is happening to me *now?*"

"Nothing of the sort," Mary told her. "It's not happening

to you at all. It's happening to your mother. And she'd get a lot better care than you can give her. Why all this fuss?"

Janet stopped sobbing, but she remained silent while the other group members asked Mary many questions. She told them that, as a young woman, she had put aside all thoughts of marriage. She had heard about families in which generation after generation suffered from the same mental condition as her mother. "I couldn't risk being the same awful problem to a child of my own," she stated.

After a dramatic reawakening of the past, whether through an uninterrupted personal narrative or the ventilation of intense feelings in some lively interchange among group members, the next session often produces an anticlimax. The dramatis personae of the last scene lurk in the wings, still recovering from the strain of their performance. They seem at times to have second thoughts about the wisdom of self-exposure. Recognizing the delicacy of their situation, their colleagues make little reference to what they have just witnessed and usually show little eagerness to take over the stage. Several sessions may elapse before any pressure for self-revelation builds up once more into a significant communication.

Consequently, it did not surprise me to hear Mary speak without any fire during the next session. Janet made no effort to get the group to focus on her problem. She was unusually quiet then and during the following meeting. As it drew to a close, I sensed that the other members of the group were embarrassed by her silence. Her failure to bring up an acute problem, after clinging to it so indecisively for many weeks, discomforted them as much as their own inability to help her resolve the matter.

In the face of Janet's silence, her unfinished business was

finally brought up for discussion during the last few moments of the session by a man in the group. His manifest desire to help her probably was an expression of his own need for help in dealing with a somewhat similar problem. At any rate, he made an awkward reference to the tendency of group members to hurt each other's feelings. Then, obviously speaking under great pressure, he continued: "For instance, I know that I am going to hurt Janet now, but maybe it will help her to hear what I am going to say. The way you carried on when Mary was talking gave me this idea, Janet. It made me feel that it wouldn't be as painful as you've been making out to yourself to have your mother in a hospital. It must be a great strain for anyone who works as hard as you do to have to manage and care for her too. There must have been times when you wanted to get rid of her."

"That's true," Janet replied. "I do have mixed feelings, all sorts of feelings about Mother leaving me. We've had some bad quarrels, and I can thank her for some of my worst mistakes. I'm used to taking the bitter with the sweet. But who knows if I'll ever find anyone to take her place? I guess I've been terror-stricken at the thought of living alone, and didn't realize it. But I've been thinking about Mary, and how she got along all those years without her mother. If she could do it and turn into such a fine person, I can live apart from my mother too. That really is the best solution for both of us."

As group members go on in this way, triggering memories and influencing each other's feelings through words and behavior, I get an amazingly different notion of human existence than when I sit in my office listening to a single patient. The more he tells me about himself, the more aware I become of the unique and highly personal aspects of his existence. When I listen to a group, especially after its members have helped each other to clear away the obstacles to self-revelation and are drifting along on the same emotional currents, I am struck by the number of psychic experiences which tie them together. As these experiences are highlighted, they seem to multiply. Realistically or symbolically, through these auditory impressions, communications of a therapy group tend to accentuate the universal and the commonplace in human existence.

If I list the main topics discussed in a session and note how the group shifted from one to the other, I find that these headings tell a story over and above the one each speaker thinks he is telling. Each helps to build up a common story. When I apply my knowledge of symbolism to the topics, what often emerges from the session are such common themes as these: Life with mother. Life with father. Struggle for their affection with brother or sister. Later relationships with peers or figures in authority. Lonely self-preoccupation and social maladjustment. Dissatisfaction with everyday reality and the endless pursuit of some elusive happiness.

As often as a theme is bandied about, continuously or discontinuously throughout one or many sessions, it never spins out twice in precisely the same manner. Each variation, delineating the common facts of life in a unique way, has its own emotional overtones. It presents a different sequence of events, different linkages between the causes and effects of psychic disturbances.

Whether realistically or symbolically, directly or tangentially, I often get strikingly different impressions of the same experience within a short period of time. Early in one session a man discussed his childhood and recalled his grief over his mother's sudden death when he was six years old.

He talked about his love for her, striking a responsive chord in one of his listeners. The second speaker told how his mother, widowed when her four children were very young, carried on through struggle and sacrifice. She had managed to send him to college, the group member said, and later had helped him through crisis after crisis. Since her recent death, he had been filled with remorse because he had never been able to convey to her his love and gratitude. The next man to speak said that his mother was living, but he had no desire to keep in touch with her. Tracing back his present indifference to feelings of being rejected as a child, he described his mother's failure to shield him from his father's anger. The fourth man focused on a night during his adolescence when, as he slept near his mother, he suddenly became panic-stricken about the danger of incest.

Life with mother in early childhood, in early manhood, in late childhood, and in adolescence. The cumulative impact of these four scenes in rapid succession induced powerful reactions in me. As each man talked, I became aware of his mother's feelings for him, of his feelings for her, and also of the feelings created in me by the communication. Before deciding what words the speaker needed to hear, I had to analyze the three sets of feelings together. Keeping track of the emotional logic of four lives almost simultaneously and providing the corrective responses which each speaker needed made me feel like the manager of a twelve-ring circus.

Things go on in the group which don't go on in everyday life. We want them to. But it is the psychic imprint of what actually has happened to each member which we search for together. In this way, eventually, we discover the unconscious purpose of our activity. The search for it is full of zest and excitement.

[5]

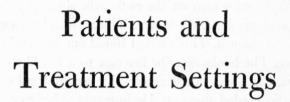

Patients and
Treatment Settings

A MAN WHO identified himself on the telephone as the uncle of a patient of mine arranged an appointment for himself and his wife to discuss the possibility of her entering treatment. When they arrived at my office at the designated hour, I was astonished to find before me a man and a woman who were in their seventies. The Clarks, as I shall call this couple, appeared to be in great distress.

A few minutes later, I learned that they had two children, five grandchildren, and had observed the fiftieth anniversary of their marriage three years earlier. I was also informed that they contemplated divorce, and had consulted a lawyer about it.

To my expression of surprise that a couple planned to separate after living together fifty-three years, the man, glaring at his wife, asserted: "She's responsible. I can't stand her picking on me any longer."

"I won't put up with him any more," Mrs. Clark retorted. "I've been miserable the last two years."

"What happened two years ago?" I inquired.

"That's when I began to find out the kind of person she is," Mr. Clark said. "We'd have broken up years ago if I'd known. But I never had the chance until I sold my business and retired. Now I'd like to get a little enjoyment out of life, and I can't get it living with her. But I'm willing to pay for her treatment. She needs it. Badly."

How had he discovered this, I asked.

"We heard a man on the radio talk about psychology and psychoanalysis. We became interested and got a couple of books about it. That's how I found out my wife's compulsive. The books describe her case to a tee. She's sick!"

Mrs. Clark was just as certain that her husband was the one who needed attention. He interrupted her to cite evidence of her "compulsive" behavior. Wouldn't I recommend that she enter treatment?

"I have one important recommendation to make to both of you," I said with a smile. "Get rid of those books on psychoanalysis."

There was no objection to reading the books and acquiring some information on the subject, I explained. The trouble was that they were torturing each other with their new knowledge. If they would stop taking each other apart, I thought that they would be able to go on living together as they had during the first fifty years of their marriage.

Before the consultation ended, they were both greatly relieved. It was obvious that they welcomed the advice. Mrs. Clark said: "I wonder why we didn't think about throwing away those books ourselves."

I haven't seen the Clarks since then. Their nephew tells

me that they have abandoned their ventures in psycho-analysis—and also their plans for a divorce.

Even when people do not exaggerate the mental distress which prompts them to consult a psychiatrist, it is often relieved through some course of action less costly in time, money, and effort than full-scale psychotherapy. I do not recommend therapy to a person who feels he can get along without it. Some professional advice or a change of scene or activity may suffice to alleviate a mild disturbance. Bruno Walter's therapeutic trip to Italy, taken on Freud's advice, is often recalled in this connection.

The termination of an unduly stressful situation has also served as a constructive alternative to psychotherapy. A violinist suffering from great anxiety and stage fright was convinced that he would need treatment if he continued his concert work. Asked whether he was deeply committed to it, he revealed that he had been invited to join the music department of a midwestern university. He felt that he would get along well there. He was philosophical about his unrealized ambition to become a great solo performer, and spoke without anxiety about giving up his concert career. I agreed that the change would be desirable. He enjoyed teaching and experienced no further need for psychotherapy.

After completing treatment for a mild disturbance, a young woman found contentment in her work and personal life for two years. Then she fell in love with a highly neurotic man. She complained of sleepless nights and of being a "nervous wreck" when she consulted me about resuming treatment. Wouldn't this help her "adjust to my future" with this man? I asked if she was certain that was what she wanted. When she admitted to some misgivings on that score, I pointed out another possibility: to forget the man. About six months later, she married someone else and embarked on the kind of future she wanted without having to wage a strenuous battle for it.

On the other hand, when psychotherapy is actually warranted, the need for it may be difficult to establish without the services of a competent diagnostician. Some persons who require professional help appear to function well at their daily tasks. The symptoms of others seem insignificant to an untrained observer; measured against the crucial problems which beset the world, their complaints are regarded as self-indulgent. One who takes the normal anxieties and stresses of everyday living in good stride may find it harder to comprehend that profound suffering and acute conflicts are often masked in such complaints and symptoms. Moreover, a person who harps on some trivial problem may have more serious ones which he does not talk about. He may prefer to believe, and give the impression, that the petty difficulty, usually the kind which he shares with "normal" people, is his only one.

One woman talked incessantly about a crack in her bedroom ceiling; it pursued her wherever she went. Yet her disorder was more painful and difficult to cure than that of the woman, also in treatment during the last world war, who was tortured by news of the destruction of the Czech village of Lidice. The topics they dwelt on were just symbols of their deep-seated disorders. The first woman was probably no more self-centered than the second, whose preoccupation with the massacre of helpless women in an unknown village gave free play to her masochistic fantasies.

Some persons with serious disorders are not aware of them. They consult a psychiatrist because they seem to be a problem to everyone else, and can't understand why. "I'm here because my wife insisted on my coming," Hans told me on his first visit. "She calls me a misfit and my boss says I'm impossible. Nothing is wrong with me, but I don't want people complaining about me."

Had he been willing to go on accepting the criticism, the loss of his job, and the breakup of his marriage, he would not have had to commit himself to intensive psychotherapy. Many persons who never recognize the inappropriateness of their behavior and the reasons for their repeated failures and disappointments manage to get by without treatment. But Hans wanted to preserve his marriage, and he had lost too many jobs to lose another without a struggle. He grasped at the suggestion that we just explore his troubles for a few months and try to find out what was causing them. In the process he recognized that he had a handicapping character disorder, and developed a great desire to overcome it. By that time he was deeply troubled about himself and convinced that psychotherapy was indispensable. The intensive study and reorganization of his personality which he needed took nearly five years to complete.

Emotional problems centering around work and love—the essentials of fruitful living—motivate most persons who turn to psychotherapy. Many of them have unreasonable fears, anxieties, and sexual problems which seriously interfere with their work or other purposeful activities. Practically every emotional disorder can now be alleviated to some extent, and many can be radically influenced to achieve permanent change, through analytic psychotherapy.

For various reasons, treatment of this kind is generally prolonged and intensive, requiring from two to five years, with from one to five sessions a week, to accomplish per-

manent improvement as well as relief. The cases of hysteria
and other relatively mild psychoneurotic conditions for
which this form of psychotherapy was originally employed
are seen infrequently today. People tend to put off treatment
as long as they can; this magnifies their problems and
lengthens the time needed to resolve them. Moreover, more
and more persons whose conditions would have consigned
them to hospitals and custodial care a decade or more ago
enter psychotherapy as it becomes increasingly effective in
influencing the most severe psychiatric disorders. Experience has led to the introduction of new techniques which
brighten the outlook for such persons; but their treatment
is still difficult and time-consuming.

Another group of patients, though usually less incapacitated, commit themselves to long periods of analytic psychotherapy because they have a great desire to realize their
maximum potentialities for achievement in life. Some of
them feel driven to make a great contribution to the general welfare, to "go places and be the best person I am capable of becoming," as one of my patients put it. They usually
have an intrinsic sense of their own capabilities; but we discuss their ambitions and hopes and come to some understanding about how much treatment is realistic. Its termination is in order when they reach the point where they need
no further help in dealing with their emotional problems, in
understanding themselves, and improving their personalities.

Cost is, of course, an important consideration. Fees are
predicated on the time spent with the patient—the regularly
scheduled visit. Those which I specify are for treatment in
New York City, where fees are probably higher than elsewhere. Persons with limited incomes may enter psycho-

therapy at psychiatric clinics, where fees range from fifty cents to fifteen dollars for an individual session and from fifty cents to ten dollars a group session. Unfortunately, many clinics have long waiting-lists.

In private practice, lay psychoanalysts charge from ten to twenty-five dollars a session for individual treatment, from five to twenty dollars for group psychotherapy. The fees of medical psychotherapists—psychiatrists and the majority of analysts—range from twenty to fifty dollars for individual sessions, and from ten to twenty-five dollars a session for the patient treated in a group. The total fees collected from the members of a group are considerably higher than what the psychotherapist receives for an individual session, reflecting the fact that group treatment is more taxing, the sessions are longer, and require more preparation and review. Many psychoanalysts beginning their practice treat patients for lower fees than those customarily charged by their more experienced colleagues.

Individual treatment, which usually entails from one to five weekly sessions, is regarded as intensive when there are at least two or three each week. Many persons, some of whom can well afford more intensive treatment, prefer to limit themselves to one or at most two a week and make satisfactory progress. Good results have been secured even with one session every two weeks. For the patient with a grave disturbance, the intensity varies with his ability to assimilate "psychological feeding" at different stages of psychotherapy.

In more typical cases, most patients who can afford it and are concerned about getting the best possible results as quickly as possible, enter the most intensive form of psychotherapy: psychoanalysis. Standard psychoanalysis, which formerly required five or six sessions a week, now involves from three to five.

However, the *therapeutic* effectiveness—the sustained benefit—of individual analytic psychotherapy does not depend primarily on the frequency of the sessions. Other things being equal, I have observed that their spacing at longer intervals leads to better results at less cost. I have advised persons with limited incomes to husband their analytic hours. For example, two hundred sessions spread over a period of five years at the rate of one a week are more beneficial than the same number held five times a week within one treatment year. It is my impression that similar principles would apply in group psychotherapy, but the effect of varying the frequency of group sessions has received little study. At the present time most groups meet once or twice a week.

The individual seeking treatment in a clinic or the office of a private practitioner is expected to meet a few minimum requirements. Those I accept are, as a rule, sufficiently oriented to reality to come and leave my office unescorted and to control their behavior during their sessions. I rarely work with a person who doesn't enter psychotherapy of his own volition. Unconscious resistances to personality change are too formidable to allow one to contend at the same time with a conscious will that is dead-set against treatment.

Occasionally, a patient changes his mind on that score. A young man whose college career was halted by a severe breakdown entered intensive psychotherapy only, I soon discovered, because of his parents' insistence that he do so. After he had threatened to tear my office apart and kill me rather than co-operate, I told him not to return unless he really wanted to be treated. He appeared a few weeks later, and there were no further interruptions in his long and arduous treatment.

Additional qualifications are usually imposed on the candidate for group psychotherapy. Membership in a regular group is not recommended for a person suffering from serious physical illness, such as heart disease or diabetes, which might interfere with his own functioning or curtail the freedom of action of other patients. He needs the greater protection afforded by the one-to-one relationship. This is also more desirable for anyone who would be exposed to emotional wear and tear because of some extreme difficulty in talking; once this has been resolved, however, group therapy may be beneficial. Alcoholics and drug addicts are among others generally excluded from mixed groups. Many of them do well in the special groups organized to deal with their respective problems, including self-help groups, such as Alcoholics Anonymous, which are not actually engaged in psychotherapy.

Psychotherapists are, as a rule, more interested in working with some types of patients than with others. Generally we get our best results with those whom we can work with most comfortably. For that reason, a patient may be confronted with special requirements, notably with respect to age and intelligence. These are not usually justified by the fact that he is too old or too lacking in "gray matter" to benefit from analytic psychotherapy. The psychotherapist may turn down the case because he feels more competent and disposed to handle younger or brighter patients.

Capacity for psychological change at a reasonably rapid rate is, nevertheless, a prerequisite. Some persons in or over their sixties can respond to psychotherapy quickly enough to warrant their entering it. Others become rigid personalities much earlier in life because they have experienced a great deal of frustration. Since flexibility does not always equate with chronological age, I assess it on an individual basis.

I have not found intelligence to be much of an issue in either group or individual treatment, because I conduct both as primarily emotional processes. It is true, of course, that an unhealthy moron cannot blossom into a healthy genius; but to refuse to treat him would seem as unnatural to me as disowning a child because he is feeble-minded. Placing patients with low intelligence quotients in a group with extremely bright ones is generally avoided; but a moderate degree of discrepancy stimulates efforts at communication and may make for a more emotional experience. I have worked with patients of low-average intelligence and found them very responsive to analytic psychotherapy, even when they didn't fully comprehend the therapeutic process.

"I didn't know I'd have to take a course in human psychology here," a woman making good headway told me. "I just wanted you to make me well." But this attitude is not limited to persons of low intelligence. An extraordinarily bright little girl said to me time and time again during her treatment: "Don't explain. Just get me better so I can leave."

More frequently, though, a highly intelligent person will regard the "psychology course"—intellectual knowledge— as all-important and fight against involving himself in the emotional experience which I try to give him. The easier it is for him to understand the therapeutic process, the more stubbornly he may fight against it. He may say he knows he will never get well, and is in treatment just to prove it, or to find out all he can about his illness.

I meet with such an attitude from time to time in patients

of superior intelligence who are highly motivated to undergo psychoanalysis. Instead of benefiting from the self-knowledge which they acquire, they tend to punish themselves with it or to become more confused. They may become absorbed in themselves to a frightening degree, or overly dependent on the treatment relationship itself. For persons who use their intellect in this way, classical psycho-analysis is not the most therapeutic procedure. They are more responsive to some modified analytic approach which will bring their intellect and emotions into better balance. Some of them do well in a group, where it is difficult to maintain an indiscriminately intellectual attitude. They are stimulated to behave more spontaneously through their exposure to the feelings of other patients.

I recall one self-absorbed woman whose group frequently commented at the start on her lack of spontaneity. She would tell the other members that she "knew too much" to behave the way they did. She reacted to their uninhibited behavior at first by sternly admonishing them to "stop this nonsense and hit reality." A year and a half later, she was engulfed in her own feelings and being taunted for acting unreasonably. More than once she was asked: "Where's that famous old common sense of yours?"

Someone about to enter psychotherapy may express a decided preference for individual or group treatment. If he does, I respect his wishes unless our mutual investigation of his complaints indicates that treatment in the setting he favors might be undesirable for him. I also follow his own plan when I am uncertain which would be better, or if the settings appear to be equally good for his treatment. I don't like to force someone who yearns for a lively party into a quiet tête-à-tête, or the reverse, unless there is some compelling reason to do so.

People planning to enter treatment frequently ask whether I think individual or group therapy would be better for them. They tend to assume that the choice of setting depends on how their case is classified, as it usually would if they were entering treatment for physical illness. However, diagnosis is less significant in prescribing a course of psychological treatment. The psychiatrist, following the same general principle applied in organic medicine, recommends the procedure which will be least taxing for the patient; but the clinical description of his condition does not by itself indicate how he can be helped most rapidly and with least stress in psychotherapy. More reliable guides are his personality and the kind of problems he has, especially those associated with talking about his feelings.

He may not know what his problems are when he first consults a psychiatrist. When I asked one woman what was troubling her she replied: "I came here to find that out." Like the infant wailing for his mother, she was distressed but didn't know why.

After spending from three to fifteen hours with a patient, exploring his complaints, I know his impressions and he gets to know mine. Our impressions don't always tally, nor do our opinions on how to produce the change which he desires. It is a good augury for the case if we agree on both points; but if we don't the preferred course will be mapped out during treatment. We are more advanced if he honestly disagrees with me than if he complies superficially with my impressions and opinions on the theory that the doctor knows best.

Richard, an accountant in his mid-thirties who suffered from anxiety attacks, consulted me about individual therapy. Since his attacks occurred in social situations, I suggested that we might begin investigating his difficulties in the group setting. He accepted the suggestion with a great show of enthusiasm.

After a few group sessions, he reported a dream about the beard he was growing. In the dream several of his office associates made some scathing comments about his shaggy appearance, and he agreed at their urging to shave off the beard. The dream ended with his being applauded for the decision.

"I suddenly remembered the dream on my way here tonight," Richard said, "and it made me very uncomfortable. Why did I tell them that I would shave off my beard? As you can see, I had no intention of doing it. I guess I just wanted to say what would please them most. But I really don't feel like saying anything about the dream. I feel very secretive tonight. I wonder why I came."

The group discussed his dream anyway. One member interpreted it to mean that Richard objected to "letting his hair down." Another interpretation was that he was determined to "cover up." The third advanced was that Richard would say anything to get people to like him. I told him that he wasn't interested in being treated but wanted to make it appear that he was.

He did not comment immediately on the interpretations. Later on, though, Richard admitted that he had felt strongly, at the start of his group treatment, that it wouldn't benefit him; and he believed in his feelings. Then why, I asked, had he agreed to it so enthusiastically?

"I faked my optimism," he replied, "because I didn't want to discourage you."

His progress became more apparent after he began to work honestly with me and his co-patients. Now he says he is getting well just to prove that he doesn't need us.

Some persons who leave the choice of treatment setting

to their therapist don't care much about the relative values of group and individual psychotherapy. One who feels that he has reached the limit of his endurance is likely to start out with the plea: Make me feel better right away. I don't care how you do it. He may also be skeptical about the value of "just talking"; or the notion of sharing attention and "letting himself go" in the presence of other patients may add to his turmoil. For the person entering treatment in this state of mind, individual psychotherapy is usually advisable. It leads to a rapid easing of his tension; this encourages him and instills in his mind the idea that talking is worth while. Improvement in behavior might have been more marked after a few months of group treatment, but that is a secondary consideration.

"My job's my life," one moderately ill woman declared during her first visit, "but I gave it up today. I just can't work any longer in this condition." When she entered treatment a week later, she remarked: "I decided to go on working now that I have someone on my team." Her expectation of getting help was not the only reason why she changed her mind. The verbal communication of her difficulties and notification that I would make an effort to help her were also beneficial. Some persons experience a surge of relief when they make their arrangements to enter treatment.

For many patients, perhaps a majority, the choice of setting is not a crucial issue. Mild neurotic conditions generally respond favorably to analytic psychotherapy, whether given individually or in a group.

I analyzed a young man who complained that his emotional disturbance prevented him from driving an automobile. I asked him if he had taken any driving lessons. He had not, he replied; he felt that he would be able to drive without them if he could get on intimate terms with his unconscious. He and his unconscious eventually became so well acquainted that he was able to recognize for himself how irrational this attitude had been. He had some driving lessons and obtained his operator's license a few weeks later. Had he been treated in a group, he would not have explored his unconscious so thoroughly; but his fantasies of circumventing the normal routines and tasks of life would have been punctured, probably more vehemently, by his co-patients.

For those who suffer from serious forms of emotional and psychosomatic illness, the choice of procedure is important and may even spell the difference between an unfavorable and a favorable outcome. In a sense, psychotherapy represents "controlled" reliving to undo the harmful effects of "natural" living. Obviously, a patient cannot "live" over his whole life in treatment. The objective is to expose him in his sessions to situations similar to those in which he developed his inappropriate attitudes and patterns of behavior, so that these may be clearly reactivated and modified as efficiently as possible.

Some situations are symbolically re-created with maximum emotional intensity, as a rule, when only one other person is present. That is why knotty problems stemming from a patient's most intimate experiences can usually be resolved more efficaciously in individual treatment. Other significant situations may be difficult to revive, or are revived only pallidly as he relates to the therapist. Family problems, such as too intense sibling rivalries or conflicts with both parents can, as a rule, be pinpointed and modified more easily in the group.

It would be relatively easy to select the right setting for persons with serious disturbances if they always conformed to the major criteria I have just outlined. They do not. For one reason or another, some of them respond poorly to the setting which is theoretically more desirable and then do substantially better in the other one. Age, special transference situations, atypical reactions, and a too intellectual approach to the therapeutic process are factors which often tip the balance in the other direction.

Children and adolescents, for example, often make more rapid progress in the shared experience. I supervised the treatment of a group of seriously disturbed teen-age girls whose therapist had previously treated all of them individually, with disappointing results. Youngsters are apt to make slow headway in the one-to-one relationship, an observation which has given rise to various explanations. I attribute it to the fact that they cannot assimilate much communication from an adult; it gives them too rich a diet. They require limited dosages of interpretation, interspersed with prolonged periods of silence. From others in their own age group, however, they can assimilate a great deal more communication.

Dramatic personality changes occurred in these eight teen-agers during the course of their group treatment. The discovery that they had similar ideas and feelings helped them to talk freely about matters which had been too exciting for them to talk about in the treatment twosome or which they had resisted talking about, perhaps out of family pride. They developed warm feelings about the group itself, and these tended to counteract the adverse effects of their faulty home life. Besides functioning well together with her peers, each girl also formed a healthy attachment to the therapist. Subsequently, they were able to get on better terms with their own parents. Two emotionally retarded members of the group also benefited substantially from the opportunity it afforded them to identify with other girls of their age.

Like the adolescent or child, an occasional adult with severe emotional problems responds to the catalytic effect of the group after having bogged down in individual treatment. Had his therapist been more adequate to meet this adult's special needs, he might not have bogged down; but that is beside the point. The patient may have found it difficult to face the therapist without undue anxiety or hostility. Another reason for failure, notably among persons brought up in a cold atmosphere, is their inability to experience strong emotions unless they can induce these in their treatment partner. With an analyst who never develops angry feelings, for example, such a patient tends to suppress his own anger. In a group, he is less inhibited, since it is easier to induce strong feelings of anger or affection in his co-patients. Their emotional reactions gradually release him from the inhibitory effects of the therapist's own attitude.

Before drawing up a plan for treatment, I try to get some idea of how well a person handles himself socially. For example, does he function without undue anxiety in company? Does he grasp what is said to him and respond readily? Is he sufficiently alert to the reactions of others to know when to stop talking?

Affirmative answers to questions such as these suggest that he is in sufficiently good contact with people to clear up his social difficulties by cultivating some new friends, joining a club, or simply by making the effort to get on better terms with his neighbors and acquaintances. The person who can do so usually spends his time more profitably concentrating on his intimate problems in the one-to-one relationship, which is harder to duplicate in life. On the other hand, if I get the impression that he is ill at ease in social situations, not very alert to what goes on around him, and obtuse to the reactions his behavior generates in others, I usually believe that he has a strong need for the group experience.

In a few instances, though, I have decided otherwise. I did so in the rather exceptional case of Andrew. This brilliant and highly egocentric man, without family ties or social life, had a history of fifteen disappointing years in individual psychotherapy. The net profit he had garnered from thousands of hours spent with a succession of competent and well-known analysts was the consolation that his treatment had prevented him from getting any worse. His last analyst decided that they had worked long enough together and suggested that Andrew might benefit from group treatment at that point. He himself expressed no preference for one procedure or the other; he said that he would comply with my recommendations. Smiling feebly, he remarked: "For a shipwrecked man like me, any life raft will do. I don't care who else is on it."

During the hours we spent exploring his problems, I had to investigate why he had done so poorly in individual treatment. He was severely depressed and further incapacitated by frequent anxiety attacks. He appeared to have a terrific need to outwit me and to demonstrate superiority. His repeated assertions that his former analysts had "talked garbage" to him gave me the impression that he had successfully fought off getting into a sincere relationship with any of them.

Andrew demonstrated that attitude of basic unforgiveness which explains why transference does not lead to cure in some cases. He was one of those persons who, having experienced some parental attitude as unpardonable, has to defeat and leave the first analyst with whom that attitude is re-experienced. Indeed, some patients do not exhaust this need until they have deprived more than one analyst of the satisfaction of curing them, usually late in treatment. The Promised Land is already in clear view when such a transference failure occurs, so I think of it as a "Moses complex."

Patients who suffer from it often do well in group treatment; their hostility to the analyst is diluted by the presence of other patients. In Andrew's case, however, I decided that his deep-seated problems required individual attention. After he had reactivated his attitude of concealed superiority on my couch and we had analyzed it together, it became clear that it was the outgrowth of his intensely rivalrous relationship with his father.

In addition to the need for individual exploration in this case, there were two other reasons why I would have hesitated to place Andrew in a group. He lived in the clouds of high finance, and it would have been difficult to find emotionally and intellectually stimulating treatment partners for him. Andrew spent his leisure hours lying in bed and indulging in sexual fantasies, but not because he lacked resources for sociable living. Every day, in fact, many people came to his executive suite in a large corporation. His problem was that the limited store of energy available to one in his emotional state was drained off by the responsibilities of his post. Since his recovery, he has been able to take on added responsibilities and to enjoy a full social schedule as well. He has also learned how to delegate responsibility sufficiently to be active in civic affairs.

Many who do go on from individual to group treatment are persons who are cut off from wholesome family and social life by force of circumstances or the restricting in-

fluence of their illness. There are others who, for various
reasons, start in a group and then enter individual treatment
or have both experiences during the same period, usually
though not necessarily with the same therapist. They com-
prise a category of patients for whom psychotherapy in
either setting is less rapid, effective, and deep-seated than
that provided, simultaneously or in sequence, in both
settings—combined treatment.

Group psychotherapy itself is, in a sense, combined treatment. The prospective group member explores his problems to some extent in private discussions with his therapist,
and may also consult him alone from time to time after
entering the group. But individual sessions of this nature
are an adjunct to the group treatment, few in number, and
are rarely conducted on a regular and systematic basis.

The transfer of a person with a severe disorder from
individual to group psychotherapy has to be carefully
timed, in his own interests and those of the other patients he
will join. He may have to undergo a great deal of "hot-
house" nurturing before he can withstand the more rigorous group climate and derive the desired benefit from it.
To give one illustration: I would hesitate to place in a
group any person with problems like those of Donald of my
first group when he entered individual treatment with me.
Were I to do so, the patient would probably oscillate between monopolizing my attention and sinking into prolonged silences. Behavior of this sort is intolerable to other
group members and exposes the offender to harmful re-
prisals.

Some painful hours in a group which he "sampled" some
months ago, out of curiosity and to please his wife, taught
one man that there are undesirable ways of committing

oneself to any form of treatment, as to any other course of action.

When he told me about this illuminating experience, Angus, a basketball coach in his mid-thirties, had been in individual psychotherapy with me nearly two years. He was emerging very slowly from a state of severe anxiety and depression.

After opening his session on the couch each week with a perfunctory account of his current activities, Angus often plied me with questions which reflected his perplexity and worry about the waywardness of his feelings. Why should they be leading him into amorous adventures with other women, he wanted to know, when he had a wonderful and loving wife? And why had he been so unwilling to have children with Betty during the five years of their marriage? Getting me to answer gave him enormous satisfaction. Since he expended most of his energy acting out his impulses in gestures and in the twistings and turnings of his lean muscular body, he had little to spare for the recall of memories. He customarily indulged in the kind of small talk which fills an inexperienced analyst with despair.

He was much more animated than usual the day after his first session in a marital group. Angus told me: "I had an interesting experience last night. I finally went with Betty to that group for husbands and wives—you know, the one she's been begging me to go to with her. You didn't recommend it, but you didn't tell me not to go, so I decided to try it out, to please her. She talked a little, but I just sat back and listened to the old-timers. One woman rambled on about the hard time her little boy was giving her. Her husband didn't open his mouth—a henpecked specimen if ever I saw one. I loathed them both when his wife described the wicked beltings she gives the child. It reminded me of a terrible beating my mother once gave me for no reason at all, and of my father's mousy attitude about everything that went on in our home. Other things that went on there came back to me, things I could never remember to tell you. I couldn't talk about them last night, but I want to do it now."

Angus attended a few more group sessions. Watching and listening to the other members seemed to satisfy his hunger for information; at any rate he did not ask for any. Nor did he give any. He was afraid to talk in his wife's presence. Consequently, the many memories stirred up by the disclosures of the other group members were not utilized therapeutically—that is, to facilitate the processes of recall and communication. The tension of being "clammed up" by his fears when he felt a growing urge to talk about his memories was more than he could endure. He insisted on leaving the group after a month. Betty never knew why. It was still her impression that he suffered from some sexual incapacity of emotional origin which had prompted him to enter individual psychotherapy.

This experience made Angus more depressed and had other adverse effects. After these were dissipated, one plus factor emerged: The group episode gave impetus to his individual treatment. He stopped asking so many questions. He became more interested in his memories and spent more time recalling them. He talked about his rearing by parents who, by mutual consent, had brought their respective love mates into their home. He came to understand his tendency to repeat their adulterous behavior, though he transgressed more discreetly with a few female companions during trips with his teams to athletic meets in other cities. He acknowledged that, even though he loved his wife, the other women were in many ways more attractive to him. He realized that he was afraid to discuss the situation with Betty, particularly her lack of physical appeal for him.

"Never again," Angus vowed when he pulled out of the group. "It's not for me." Now he understands why I did not approve of his entering the marital group at the time he did so, and agrees that membership in a congenial group when he is ready for it would probably accelerate his progress.

On the couch some patients, especially those who are overcharged with the significance of a long and intimate relationship with one person, give me few clues to peculiarities in their behavior in their daily work or social encounters. This was true of Nila, an emotionally withdrawn young commercial artist who entered treatment shortly after her father's death. Her mother had died in childbirth, and Nila and her twin brother were brought up by their temperamental and domineering male parent. It was an experience which blinded her to any real awareness of other people. In her weekly sessions during three years of individual treatment, she scarcely touched on her lack of friends and her difficulties in getting on with her associates in the advertising agency where she worked.

For one so immature, growth involved getting to know what other people thought and felt. I therefore suggested that she complete her psychotherapy in a group. She agreed that this might be beneficial.

Nila's objectionable behavior showed up as soon as she got together with other patients. Alone with me, she had been highly respectful. She had humbly solicited my opinions as if she herself had no convictions of her own. With them she acted in an egotistical and domineering manner. She quickly made it plain that she had strong convictions on every subject which came up, and she attempted to impose them on her treatment mates.

Much as she tried, though, they did not allow her to control and drive them. They usually let her have her say and then spelled out her arrogance and distorted attitudes. The impact of their criticism and pressure on her to function more democratically eventually wore her down. In due time they also complimented her on the gradual improvement in her behavior; but no one was as excited and impressed with the change as Nila herself. At times, she expressed frank agreement with their criticism or even anticipated it.

"Let's make this be-kind-to-Nila night," she said at the beginning of a session. "I know I deserve your criticism, but it will digest better with a few sweet words. I could use them now that I'm getting ready to go to the hospital. I'm making my will and putting my affairs in order for better or worse."

This opened up another lively debate on Nila's need to be operated on for a gastric ulcer. Her references to it had been interpreted by one of her co-patients as an unconscious plea for more merciful treatment. Others had a different opinion. They sized up the case as one of *mania operativa passiva* in a woman who had met up with a surgeon with *mania operativa activa*. They argued so eloquently for this diagnosis that it was unnecessary for me to do more than propose my customary settlement for disputes of this nature: consultations with one or more competent diagnosticians. Nila consulted two. She reported a week later that both had assured her she did not need an operation. She sounded disappointed, but that ended the matter.

For about a year, she underwent a leveling experience which was rather stormy. However, it was not too shocking for her. Her childhood had conditioned her to blow up little tiffs with her father into tremendous explosions and even to get some hysterical enjoyment from them. I evaluated her occasional reports that she had cried all night over some unkind remark made about her in a session within the context of that conditioning. Actually, she was not harmed by the many barbs directed at her because she had no difficulty talking when she was tense or angry.

I have to make a distinction between normal growing pains and the psychological damage which can be incurred through such an experience. Can the group member talk freely when he gets angry or labors under some other strong emotion? That is a crucial consideration. I am alert to the possibility that a patient is being damaged if he withers mutely instead of reacting strongly to some verbal sideswipe.

Thomas, an engineer, had been in group treatment with another analyst before he consulted me, and at his request I put him in one of my groups. Although he was a convivial person in the company of a friend or two, a mildly disparaging remark from someone in a position of authority usually floored him. Out of a feeling of worthlessness, he tended to agree with anyone who criticized him, however unjustifiably.

In the group, Thomas customarily responded to unfavorable remarks about him by retreating into a depressed silence. He seemed especially sensitive to expressions of hostility, and to censure which he felt was merited or which related to some aspect of his functioning which gravely concerned him. However deeply the criticism bit, Thomas never got angry. It became necessary to remove him from the group. I kept him in individual psychotherapy until he was able to ventilate his emotions freely.

Psychotherapy is bound to delineate sharply and, in some cases, even to intensify the difficulties patients have about talking. One man complained that having to talk was ruining his analysis. The opposite point of view was voiced by a woman who couldn't stop talking. To do so, she felt, would be like ordering an expensive dinner in her favorite restaurant and then not eating it.

In individual treatment, I often have to modify my procedures considerably to cope with such extreme attitudes. One man who entered psychotherapy after electric-shock treatment was too depressed and confused to complete a sentence during his first year of treatment. I respected his need for prolonged periods of silence; these alternated with "lecture periods," during which I talked to him about books and plays and various other subjects. When we got to the heart of his emotional conflict, he recognized his unconscious fear that disclosures about himself would be as traumatic for him in treatment as they already had been in life. However, the more I talked to him, the greater his urge to talk to me. Though I did most of the talking during the first two years, he did most of it during his third year.

As a group leader, I am rarely placed in a situation where I have to talk at length. Group process resolves talking problems automatically because of the tempering effects which group members have on each other. Interchange with more gregarious persons oils the tongue of their too silent partner; his presence, in turn, tends to inhibit any overtalkative member. The objective is not time-sharing, session after session, on a mathematical basis, but versatility in talking. The group member should be able to be voluble or reserved, as he prefers.

The outstanding beneficiary of the therapy group is the person whose outer life is emotionally impoverished, either because he lacks social contacts or does not enjoy them. An isolated or friendless person, one who drifts from job to job or doesn't work at all, usually gets a better foothold on life in the group. The real or imaginary stigma under which he labors disappears in the group setting.

It also serves as a forensic training ground where a person who has never enjoyed a real argument in life can become proficient in countering verbal thrusts and parries. To explode in anger at someone else when he feels like it, or to be the butt of another person's anger, gives him a much-needed feeling of importance. The give-and-take of words in a well-functioning group affords a great deal of exercise in "blowing off steam."

Expressions of interest and warm feelings from other patients are a first-rate antidote for loneliness. When group members discover that they have common experiences or interests, or similar feelings about many things, they tend to lose their sense of isolation. The encouragement they get from their co-patients buoys up their own confidence in getting well. Another bracing tonic is the realization that one helps others by exchanging thoughts and feelings with them.

"It is most blessed to give while one is receiving," a woman declared in a group session.

Being helpful often enhances the self-esteem and dignity of persons in group treatment. As one man put it: "I'm not a nothing any more. If telling you what I feel helps you, it makes me a first-class person."

The group itself as a functioning entity gets to have a meaning for persons with few social contacts. Between sessions they think about the most recent disclosures of their co-members, wonder how they are faring and what they will report at the next meeting. They feel a need to talk and listen to each other even if they have no pressing problems to report. The regularity of the sessions gives them a sense of security.

I got my first inkling of this when an out-of-town engagement forced me to cancel a meeting of my first group. Most of the members never missed any sessions unless they were physically ill, and not always then. One woman arrived at my office one evening with a high fever. When I reminded her that a temperature of 100° or higher was a cue to stay home, she said: "I didn't take mine. I was afraid to find out what it was."

At the meeting following the one I had canceled, group members complained about my having deprived them of a session. I invited them to give full expression to their annoyance. Later I repeated my original apology. I would not have canceled the meeting, I explained, if it had not been very important for me to be elsewhere at the time. I pointed out that I had lost most by the cancellation. It saved them some money. I was the only financial loser.

My statement provoked a lively argument. Several group members felt that not having to pay me didn't fully compensate them for the loss of the session. Reference was made to the group rule that a member paid his fee for any session he did not attend unless the group as a whole decided otherwise. "We didn't sanction your absence," one member told me. When she was absent, another one stated, it was bad enough missing the session, but she had to pay the fee in addition.

"Fork over some money for that session you missed," she called back to me as she left my office.

From time to time I have to remind group members that they have come only to communicate their emotions, not to act on them. Some of them, as I have already illustrated, want to convert the test materials in the laboratory of verbal interchange into the stuff of real life.

It is made clear that contacts outside the sessions interfere with therapy. "Kaffeeklatches, riding home together, and other contacts may be enjoyable," I tell them, "but they are ruled out because they won't make you better."

Some group members form social relationships anyway. A few marriages have also taken place, though not among members of my groups. However, a patient of mine occasionally reports that he has telephoned another group member, sent him a birthday card, or visited him at home. Violations also have come to my attention in other ways. For example, a group member who faithfully obeys the rule will report seeing some of the others arriving or leaving my office together.

A woman who reported such an incident to me was advised by other patients to forget it. A man in the group asked her: "Don't you know he's like the cop who stops and warns you and then lets you go without a ticket?"

Could I do more about the group members' defiance of the regulations? Not very much, short of refusing to continue treating them. I might conceivably do this if these violations were consistently destructive for the group as a whole or indicated to me that it could no longer function therapeutically. Otherwise, I have no way of enforcing the rules I lay down even if I wanted to do so. I don't. I am not interested in running my patients' lives for them. All I want to do is to understand them and help them improve their functioning. My analysis of their reactions to the rules is part of the therapeutic process.

As general guides to beneficial conduct, of course, the rules of a group contribute to its members' recovery in the same way that traffic laws contribute to public safety. At

times, though, the breaking of one group rule or another
has turned out to be therapeutic. Herman, a lonely young
man who felt inferior to the other members of his group,
invited one of them to his apartment. The visitor's enthusiastic comments at the next session on his host's skill in
ceramics, an avocation Herman had not mentioned to his
co-patients, gave his ego a great boost. Herman's own
report of the visit gave me wonderful material for analysis.
The disclosure of this "illegal" fraternization shocked a
group member who appeared to get no place in treatment.
He obeyed every rule to the letter but checked most of his
feelings. Blind compliance was one of his unconscious resistances to communicating and understanding his feelings.

In forming a group, I put together persons who will be
able to develop intense emotional reactions to each other.
The sexes get equal representation. The patients are usually
alike in some respects and different in others. Divergence
in personality structure blended with reasonably compatible backgrounds—in education and occupation, for
example—usually make it possible for group members to
relate well to each other and to function efficiently as a
unit. With diverse personalities represented, interchanges
go on among the calm, the excitable, those who easily
arouse excitement, and others who tend to check it. As
they stimulate each other in different ways, group process
is mobilized.

I have the impression that emotions would also get
churned up therapeutically if the formula I have just outlined were reversed. In other words, a group could be composed of persons with similar personalities and different
backgrounds.

It would be fascinating to form a group of highly aggressive personalities—"top dogs" in various fields with

conflicting interests. A police chief interacting in a therapy group with a gang leader, or an industrial tycoon with the head of a labor union, could certainly stir up a great deal of hatred. If they also developed love for each other and learned how to prevent any of their feelings from seriously interfering with their functioning in the sessions, I would know that they were having a therapeutic experience together. This could be the supreme test of the power of group psychotherapy.

[6]

An Afternoon in
My Office

A GREAT DEAL has been written about the "fifty-minute hour," but its complement is rarely mentioned. Nevertheless, the ten-minute period which precedes the session proper is an important interlude for both analyst and analysand.

For the latter, it affords a necessary transition from external realities to the session on the couch ahead of him. He relaxes by himself in the waiting-room, free to read or meditate. That was where one busy executive I analyzed, who could not recall working, relaxing, or even taking a brief walk without company, discovered the pleasure of being alone. He attributed his recovery to those interludes beyond the reach of callers or telephone. "You spoiled it all by inviting me inside," he once told me. "That started my trip to the torture chamber. But I learned a great deal about myself before you opened the door."

For the analyst, the ten-minute interval is a time for contemplation, planning, and attending to personal needs. Physically it gives him a seventh-inning stretch. In his chair behind the couch during a session, he rarely changes his position because any movement of his body, though scarcely noticed when he is seated at his desk conducting a group, is apt to be disturbing to the patient alone with him. Occasionally I take advantage of the interval between sessions to make a telephone call or to read a special-delivery letter detailing a patient's afterthoughts on a recent discussion. But by and large the interlude between analytic hours is devoted to thoughts, note-taking, and preparation for the next case.

I lengthen the interval of solitary preparation to thirty minutes before a group session. Its approach in the late afternoon or evening signals a change of pace in the day's activity. After hearing my office bell sound just once hour after hour, six or eight rings in succession tap out a new message—more insistent and challenging. By that time my intimate and relatively controlled meetings with the "only child" have become routine, and the presence of sextuplets or octuplets provides a welcome antidote.

In the early years of my practice, I spent considerable time after my last treatment session writing a summary of the day's activity. Comparisons of cases and thoughts about the differences and similarities in their handling summoned patients together in my mind. To summon some of them together physically as well, toward the end of the day, is a more vivid and taxing procedure. The emotional interchanges that have gone on, one at a time, in a long series of person-to-person interviews are recapitulated and compressed into one and a half or two hours of group treatment. To convey the nature of the combined experience for the analyst, I shall describe an afternoon's activity in my office. It included a consultation with a junior colleague, sessions with two individual patients, and one with a group.

My first appointment was with a young psychiatrist, whom I shall introduce as Dr. Asa Felix. Before he arrived, I thought back to our first consultation a few weeks earlier and wondered what had happened to him since then in his dealings with an attractive young secretary in his first group. She was known to me only as Annette.

Dr. Felix believed that his good looks were creating some difficulty in his practice. That had become apparent from our first discussion. I had been rather amused by his casual reference to Annette's impending withdrawal from the group. To his regret, a problem had arisen which he thought was insoluble.

Asked what his problem was with her, he had replied: "It's not my problem but hers. She has told me it would be unwise for her to continue. She intimates that she has fallen in love with me."

"Many women have expressed love for me," I had told him. "As far as I can tell, it helped their treatment. Why should the love of one woman worry you?"

"It doesn't," Dr. Felix had replied. "It doesn't bother me because I know I don't exist for her as a person. She is just transferring feelings."

"So you don't think she has feelings of love for you?"

"Not for me. She just thinks she has. She is transferring her feelings for her parents."

"Didn't she really love them?"

"She did. She has always had a great longing to know them," he had said. "They were both killed in an automobile accident when she was a child. I don't deny the reality of her love, but she doesn't love me."

"Why not? You say she has the same feelings for you now."

"I might feel she loved me if she knew me as an actual person," he had asserted, "but since she really doesn't know me at all, she is just conveying feelings for her parents. I would be glad that she developed such a strong transference so quickly if that was all there was to it. But she is making personal propositions or, at least, hinting at them. She started out by calling me a stick-in-the-mud because I wouldn't sit with her over a cup of coffee. Now she threatens to drop out of the group if I don't demonstrate a little feeling for her by seeing her socially. This is more transference love than I can deal with."

"It sounds more like transference hatred," I had told him. "Isn't she trying to knock you out of your analytic role? She came to you for treatment, and now she is making personal demands that would make it impossible for you to continue the analytic relationship. But how do you feel about her advances? Is something going on between the two of you?"

This was impossible, Dr. Felix had insisted. He had no feelings about Annette's advances. But he was concerned about my suggestion that she might be trying to make a fool of him.

"Thanks for mentioning it," he had remarked as our discussion ended. "I'm going to investigate the possibility."

I was wondering if he had already done so when Dr. Felix arrived for his consultation. A few minutes later, he briefed me on subsequent developments. "I spoke to her before the next group session and asked her what she was up to," he said. "She protested at first that she really loved me; that was the sole reason for her threats. I told her I thought her little game had gone far enough. I didn't budge from that position.

"Finally she gave in. 'You looked pretty vulnerable to me,' she told me. 'I could see that I appealed to you. It would have been a feather in my cap to get you to say so. But how did you figure this out?' She seemed relieved about it—not rejected, as I had expected her to feel, but glad to be understood. Then she asked me not to kick her out of the group. She still thought I was wonderful, she said, but she wouldn't break up her treatment to have an affair with Adonis himself."

He must have been naïve to assume that he could get away with an ostrich defense, Dr. Felix went on. Now that his head was out of the sand, he could see that he actually did find Annette very attractive. This had disturbed him because he thought he wasn't supposed to have such feelings for his patients. "My idea has been that I'm just supposed to analyze them," he added. "If I allowed myself to have feelings for this girl, wouldn't these interfere with her treatment?"

"As you know," I told him, "analysts have different views on this subject. My own experience is that feelings help rather than hinder in analytic work. What interferes with it are tendencies to behave improperly. If you're well insulated against acting impulsively, I believe you will find that your feelings for your patients will help you understand them and give them the therapeutic experience they need."

"Do you reveal hostile feelings to your patients?" Dr. Felix asked.

"I don't reveal any of my feelings, as a rule, unless it is part of my general strategy to let a patient know that I have particular feelings for him. I did tell one woman this morning that she would probably choke on her next cigarette. I make such statements to her, not to express hostility, but because they are helping her resolve her great terror of sudden death."

The idea that he had a right to have feelings for patients, as long as he acted in accordance with what was best for analytic process, would make him feel more comfortable in working with them, my young colleague remarked. He was fast learning that they often developed desires for other things besides understanding and emotional relief in treatment. It disconcerted him to hear them say so frequently that they felt like leaving treatment.

"When I heard patients talk that way at the beginning of my practice, I used to wonder how it was possible to work with such unreliable people," I told him. "That wasn't as serious, though, as when they said they had decided to drop out. Some did that too. But their attendance records improved fantastically as I improved in my handling of them. When they feel free to discharge in language the feelings of frustration and resentment created by the analytic relationship, I have found that they rarely need to discharge these feelings in action. Still, it no longer surprises me if a patient who never misses a session reveals that he feels like giving up."

During the next hour I sat behind the couch while a slight dark-haired woman in her middle thirties, a recent divorcée, spoke resentfully about her closest friends. When she was with them, Mabel said, she pretended that her teaching career filled her life, but she explored her problems honestly in treatment. She wanted to understand why the marriages of her associates were successful and why her own had failed. She was deeply jealous of their marital happiness. All her difficulties would be resolved, she felt, if she could find a man who wanted the love she could offer. Certainly, there was someone in the world for her, but where was he?

She paused suddenly after asking that question as if a thought had suddenly struck her. Then she asked me: "Can't you help me find a nice husband?"

I asked her to describe the person she was looking for. She mentioned several traits which she regarded as desirable in a man. Exploring her specifications with her, I asked her a series of questions. Eventually she brushed off my queries with some impatience. "You know the kind of person I want. A man like you would be fine."

How would I go about finding him? In her opinion, that would not be too difficult. I must be acquainted with a man who was marriageable and would appeal to her.

How would I introduce her to him? She made various suggestions about how they might meet, and earnestly tackled the queries which I interposed. Finally she gave up. She would try to think of a more suitable plan before the next session.

But she changed her mind before leaving the office. "Forget about it. It will be less trouble to find a man for myself."

That statement was encouraging. She was a woman who had little confidence in her ability to do things for herself. Her self-esteem mounted during my serious and lengthy consideration, which made it clear to her that I liked her and felt she deserved a worthy husband. My failure to satisfy her request immediately mobilized her resentment. She resolved not to rely on me. She felt more capable of handling the mission herself.

The ring of my bell linked my afterthoughts on Mabel with a series of associations about the patient who had just entered the waiting-room. He'd make a wonderful husband for Mabel, the thought suddenly occurred to me. Then I dismissed it. She would do a better job of selecting a husband without my interference. Daniel, a manufacturer in his early forties, was close to recovery from a severe depression. For the first time in his life, he entertained thoughts of marriage and raising a family; but there was little likelihood that he would solicit my help in finding a mate. As I opened the door to admit him, I wondered whether he would make a fresh bid for sympathy that afternoon or demonstrate his healthier new attitude about himself.

His deep sighs as he settled himself on the couch gave the answer. His mood was bleak. He talked glumly for half an hour about chronic problems in his business before the reason for his cheerless attitude became clear.

A few hours earlier he had addressed a convention of a trade association in which he had been active before his illness. In accepting an invitation to speak at the meeting, he had hoped to make his business colleagues dramatically aware of his improved functioning. But he was convinced that he had bungled the opportunity. A few persons had complimented him on the talk, but only "out of politeness," he said. It had been badly organized, and he had neglected to tell the two most amusing anecdotes saved for the occasion. Other speakers made a much better impression. The more he thought about what had happened, the more miserable he felt. He should have given some thought to his remarks and rehearsed them before the meeting. Daniel paused at that point. He appeared to be soliciting some response from me.

"Do you mean to say you gave such an important talk without preparation?" I reproached him. "A man of your prominence and experience. I'm surprised at you."

The vehemence with which I said this seemed to startle

him. The last thing he had expected from me was criticism; he thought he had given himself more than enough.

"Why should you be surprised?" he countered. "Sometimes it's much better to speak extemporaneously. I didn't prepare this talk because I usually do better when I don't."

His counterattack was my signal to proceed. "Well, this is one time when you muffed it. Let this be a lesson to you. You trusted to luck and you were a rank failure."

"Come now, I never said it was as bad as that. After all, some people praised me." Daniel's self-esteem was rising.

"Just a few old cronies," I went on. "But they weren't so enthusiastic either. Did anyone say you were a sensation?"

The question made him indignant. "Who wanted to be a sensation? There were other speakers. It would have been poor taste for me to hog the attention."

Each time I attacked, he retaliated. His counterattack became more and more heated. Finally he blew up: "Enough, enough. What have I done to get your bowels in such an uproar? Why did you get involved in my business anyway? You're just my analyst."

"All you ever want is to be attacked; you just beg for it. I gave it to you and now you feel better."

Daniel agreed with this interpretation. It gave him fresh insight into his behavior. His gloom was gone. He left my office pleased and invigorated with new understanding of himself.

One of the first lessons I learned from patients like Daniel is that sympathy usually makes them more depressed. To treat them successfully, I have to remove the obstacles which prevent them from getting angry at me. Since most of these obstacles had already been removed in his case, my exaggerated reflection of his toxic attitude made it difficult for him to maintain it that afternoon; instead, he turned the attack on me. After this new pattern of behavior was fully established, I rewarded him with an emotional interpretation.

The feelings of irritation and annoyance which Daniel induced were mobilized for the maneuver I engaged in. It would not have been convincing without them. Early in his treatment, however, when he was very sick and irritated with himself, it would not have been therapeutic to display my feelings for him. These had served only as a source of information during the many hours of quiet study while I figured out the key to his personality: his unconscious need to prove he was helpless in order to get "mother's" love by making her sorry for him. Now that I understood this problem, I used my feelings when he attacked himself to demonstrate to him that he was far from helpless. He counterattacked successfully, putting me in my place and winning the argument on rational grounds.

Even at that late stage of treatment, I did not join him in his self-attacks unless he invited a response. That was the cue, and I had to act quickly, as in that session, when it came. Moreover, I did not continue my chiding unless he started to counterattack immediately. The quality of our relationship usually made this possible. His knowledge that I would accept anything he felt like saying helped him to face my criticism and return it.

After Daniel's departure, I made my usual preparations for the group session, which would start in half an hour. I took out six of the light modern chairs stacked in my closet, and moved my couch closer to the wall. The grouping of the chairs around my desk brought into focus the three women and three men who had sat in them on that afternoon of the week for about a year.

Carter often took the chair nearest the waiting-room. It was usually the only one vacant when he arrived a minute or two late after making the cross-town trip from his editorial office. He was thirty-five, newly wed, and disappointed.

Edna, an art teacher, might sit next to him, but that was less certain. Being true to form meant, in her case, acting impulsively. I recalled how she had jumped up during the last session and offered to exchange places so that Inez could sit next to Frank. This brought Edna closer to Kent but did not make him more aware of her presence. A little later she exclaimed: "I ought to have my head examined for coming here each week. I should be spending my time in groups of two looking for a husband."

Frank, who often sat at her right, shouted at Edna at times as if she were out of easy hearing distance. A broker in his early forties with a jealous wife and a frail teen-age son, he was just beginning to acknowledge that he had problems.

Hortense, who usually took the next chair, was the middle-aged widow of a college professor who was trying to find out what to do about her loneliness. Her attitude toward the other five members was gentle and somewhat maternal.

Next to her sat Kent, a lawyer who couldn't do with or without women. The three in the group irritated him.

Inez, girl Friday to a theatrical producer, had little time left for her family. She couldn't get along well with her husband and didn't know what to do about it.

Once the chairs were arranged, I pulled back the drapes which had shut out the scenes and sounds of the outside world during most of the day. To further brighten my office, where one seventy-five-watt bulb had glowed dimly all day, I turned on several lamps. Then my ventilating equipment was set in motion. Having thus prepared the room in a few minutes, I returned to my desk to prepare myself for the session.

I looked forward to it with special eagerness that afternoon, because the group had not met for two weeks. Early in the last session Kent had canvassed his co-patients about taking a week's recess over the Christmas holidays. They agreed, and all but Hortense seemed enthusiastic about skipping a session. Since I was not asked, I did not inform them that I had intended to call off the session myself.

Had they recognized that this was my intention and deliberately reversed the situation as an unconscious expression of their resentment about the frustrations they were undergoing? I had no way of knowing, of course, but I often operated on the assumption that they knew what I was planning. This assumption gave much more meaning to Kent's proposal and the eagerness with which it was accepted. I was relieved at not having to cancel the session myself; but why, I wondered, had they not taken the trouble to ask me how I felt about it?

In the minds of the group members, I was associated with the group rule: no physical contact or action in the sessions, just talk with feeling. They felt a great need to eliminate me, along with the rule. The resentment of Inez took a more extreme form. Like the patient Dr. Felix had discussed just a few hours before, she expressed the attitude: Love me or I will leave the group.

Her disclosures about herself symbolized this attitude. At the beginning of treatment she had talked about her husband as if she were tied to him for life. Now she talked as if he were of no consequence. For example, he wished to buy a house in the suburbs. She would not budge from their centrally located apartment, and her daughter would not be forced to change schools. Living in the city had been good enough for her parents, Inez said, so it was good enough for her. She preferred to remain in the neighborhood where she had lived as a child.

"Why do you mention so many things from your past?" Edna had asked her.

"I'm talking about my future, and it's about time I started working on it. Jack can move out—alone. I hope he does. We don't agree on anything any more. I want a divorce, but the group is keeping me from getting one. I want action, and that means leaving the group."

"You want to blackmail us into being nice to you," said Edna, who always wanted Inez to leave. Hortense, whom Inez ignored, wanted her to remain. The idea of her leaving when she was so in need of treatment gave Carter an ominous feeling. Frank didn't share it. He thought it would be good for the group if she left. He'd like to make sure they got a very good-looking girl to take her place. Kent speculated that Inez might be talking about leaving because he hadn't cottoned to her.

He added: "There's not much point to your remaining since you feel so free to ignore the rules of the group. Maybe you'll stop that vulgar gum chewing if you leave."

"Perhaps she just wants to prove she can leave because she knows we're against it," said Carter. "You know you shouldn't leave, Inez, until it's approved."

"Maybe Dr. Spotnitz does approve it," Frank spoke up next. "Maybe he even planned it."

"Did you?" Edna asked me.

I ignored Frank's statement, but Edna's question gave me the opportunity I wanted to talk. I reminded Inez that, instead of verbalizing her feelings during the session, she chewed gum whenever she felt tense. "That is typical of your defiance here, but that's all right," I went on. "You have to leave, even though you haven't accomplished what you came for."

"Yes I have," she contradicted. "I've found out how to handle my husband. I know how to work it out so he'll leave me."

I had the feeling at that moment that nothing I might say would keep her in the group, but the situation required that I let her know I accepted the idea that she might leave. I told her: "You should not remain unless you make up your mind to become a real member of this group and behave like one."

"Please try to persuade her to remain," Hortense pleaded, not realizing that this would have the opposite effect. Carter seconded her request.

Deferring to them, I asked Inez: "Could you be talked into staying on?" As she shook her head, I went on: "That's what I thought."

"Don't worry, Hortense. I'm sure he has a good candidate to take her place. He'll never let this group break up." Frank's sardonic remark reflected his own resentment.

Inez's formal leave-taking at the end of that session, I recalled, had presented me with several alternatives. One was to tell her that, if she withdrew at the time, she was not to return. I decided against it; in my opinion it would have increased her determination to leave. I might, on the other hand, have asked her to remain. That would have given her a triumphant moment, but it would also have made it all the more humiliating for her to return later if she changed her mind. I responded to her good-by with equanimity.

I remembered how glumly Hortense looked at the unoccupied chair in the circle at the beginning of the next session. "I'm glad she's not coming," Edna said with a note of triumph. A moment later, to the great surprise of everyone but myself, Inez walked in and seated herself as usual.

"Well, here I am," she spoke with a show of casualness. "Edna would have baked a cake if she'd known I was coming. Don't ask me; I'll explain it. The morning after I said good-by to you, I woke up with a horrible feeling. It dawned on me that I'd left the group. That night I dreamt about visiting my parents. The house was full of friends and relatives. An uncle I hadn't seen for years came up and greeted me; he teaches psychology in California."

Her dream then became very peculiar, Inez continued. Her uncle followed her to another room and started to make love to her. She whispered to him: "Be careful. The others will see us." Later, she decided that the dream was about the group. "I think my uncle was Dr. Spotnitz," she added.

"Anyway, I called him up the next day and asked if I could come back. All he said was 'yes.' He sounded so bored. I was very disappointed. I had hoped he'd punish me by saying I couldn't, or by making it harder for me to come back."

"Why should I punish you?" I asked her. "You haven't missed a single session."

"Tell us why you really came back," Carter urged her.

"I thought a lot about something Dr. Spotnitz said last week—that I'd never really been a member of the group. I made up my mind to return and be one."

Her dream signified that she wanted affection from me. I symbolized the man who was willing to accept her and let her do what she felt like doing. Permitting her to come and go as she pleased made her feel loved.

While other group members responded to the frustrations of group process by smoking a good deal, Inez gratified herself by chewing gum during the sessions. "Some of
you smoke or chew gum to relieve your tensions instead
of talking," I had told them early in treatment. "You're
free to do what you want about this outside, but here these
practices interfere with communication." Since the others
smoked only occasionally after that, later references to this
resistant behavior were addressed specifically to Inez. She
continued to chew with grim determination following her
"return" to the group. The fact that she had not voluntarily given up the habit suggested that I had not analyzed it
successfully.

Once I told her that she slid gum into her mouth whenever she felt anxious. "Don't you think it's about time to
find out if you can handle your anxiety without it?" She
agreed that she could, but after a few sessions she gave up
the effort. Though she seductively offered to stop later, to
please Kent, expressions of disapproval from other members went unheeded. Eventually they ceased to comment
on her defiance.

My notes on the last four sessions reflected the various
changes in my approach to this problem. At the first of
these meetings Carter, looking very depressed, informed
the group that he had quarreled with his wife but couldn't
talk about it. Inez spoke up next: "I can't talk about my
difficulties now either. It's impossible for me to explain
to you people how I feel."

"What would you say if you could talk to us?" I asked
her.

She glared at me. "It's you I hate at this moment."

"Take another piece of gum, Inez," I urged as she opened
her handbag.

After extracting her gum from it, and taking a piece for herself, she invited her co-patients to join her. All but Carter accepted gum from her; he lighted a cigarette instead. An unconscious bond of sympathy momentarily gripped them, I recalled, as they chewed and smoked together. That was the first time they had deliberately engaged, as a unit, in the same pattern of resistant behavior.

Kent was the first to remark on it. "I guess we were all collaborating with Inez and Carter," he said. "Even Hortense, who thinks it's so barbaric."

"I was doing something for Inez," she said.

"Your first rebellion," Frank reminded her. "Did you realize what you were doing?"

"After I started to chew, it occurred to me I shouldn't be doing it," Hortense replied, looking directly at me. "But then I realized that you aren't God."

Later in the session, I urged Inez to take some more gum. "Why don't you see if you can't chew throughout the session?" She supposed that I was trying to stimulate her to do the opposite. In a sense I was, though simply in the process of trying to free her from the need to chew in the sessions.

"I have to be free to chew or not to chew in this group," she said. "I'm not going to do what you tell me." That was the only subject she discussed that afternoon.

The others had helped her chew gum, I pointed out, but they had not helped her talk in an emotionally significant way.

A week later I took a radically different approach. When Inez took out her gum I asked: "May I have some too?"

"This is the nicest thing that ever happened to me," she smiled as we chewed gum together. "It's strange that it happened today. I decided just a little while ago that I chew gum because I feel so lonely."

If true, that was important information, and the feeling of companionship which Inez conveyed seemed to confirm it. Chewing gum with her, which helped to resolve her feeling of loneliness, made me aware that this feeling was, for her, an obstacle to co-operative communication which had to be cleared away.

As usual, my attention to Inez made Edna feel jealous and inferior. She complained that I was neglecting her. She refused Inez's offer of gum and handed me a cigarette. For a moment I smoked and chewed simultaneously.

That was a beginning. I worked further on the problem during the next session by telling Inez that her gum chewing still worried me. She wanted to do it, she said, just because I didn't want her to.

"I don't know why she should stop," Frank declared. "You are demanding too much of her."

"This is a voluntary thing," I said, "but it is important to find out why you insist on doing something just because I don't want you to do it."

"I feel worse than when I started treatment," Inez complained. "I want you to help me. I won't chew gum if you'll do what I want."

She was supposed to be helped through understanding, not through personal gratification, I explained. Perhaps she felt lonely because so much hatred was expressed in the group. I asked: "Why have you people permitted yourselves to be gripped by a wave of hostility?"

Inez chewed when she felt lonely, she said, because she was convinced that it was impossible for people to love her. She associated this feeling with memories of her rage and fright at the birth of her younger sister.

She resented the loss of her parents' attention at that time because it made her feel unloved. Her consequent resentment over her sister's birth implanted feelings of guilt in her. Now she felt that she was not deserving of love because of guilt and hostility generated in her by lack of attention in the group.

Kent and Edna objected to my giving Inez so much individual attention. Coming to my defense, she said I was doing it because she had asked me to help her.

"Inez is the only one of you who consistently behaves with defiance," I explained. "You have all permitted her to go on doing this, and I'd like to know why you don't object to it."

She had started to chew gum, Inez said, as a senior at high school. The other girls in her class, most of them older than herself, drank and smoked. She did not enjoy doing either. Chewing gum became her own badge of sophistication.

"It gave you a feeling of security, didn't it?" I asked. "It helped you in your relationships with boys."

It made her closer to them, Inez stated. Even in the group she felt superior to the two women, more on a level with the men.

"If you had good relationships with the women, you would feel on their level too," I said.

"That's your fault," Inez complained. "The way you are treating us, you have us women hating each other."

They might not have expressed so much hatred and resentment, it was true, if I had not been working primarily up to that time to clear away the obstacles to the release of their hostile feelings. On the other hand, of course, they experienced little tension in the sessions. The only recent evidence of it was in Inez's compulsive gum chewing. She still had a great deal of difficulty verbalizing hostility; primarily, I suspected, it was hostility originating in her relationship with her mother. I would have to continue to work on this. But the time had come to work chiefly on the group's resistances to the expression of positive feelings.

The bell had already sounded out the message of two arrivals; it would soon be time for the session to commence. Having reviewed my notes and formulated my immediate objectives, I now had to consider how I should function during the session. When I kept quiet, the members of this group generally mobilized a great deal of hostility. When I was more communicative, they usually became more affectionate. Hence, a good deal of talking might be in order. But the exact amount of verbal feeding to be provided would depend on how much they wanted. Their own attempts to establish contact with me would determine whether I spoke at length or said little. To the extent to which they made it possible for me to participate, I decided, I would focus primarily on securing the verbal release of feelings of love.

It was time for the session to begin. I opened the door to my waiting-room—the signal to begin.

The first to walk in were Hortense and Edna. They talked about missing the group and being eager to see the others again. Edna, just back from Mexico, described her visits to art galleries and silver shops.

Carter, earlier than usual, complimented the women on their appearance but expressed regret that he didn't feel what he was saying. He described his visit to his family upstate as an old-fashioned holiday. His wife had complained of neglect because he had spent much time there visiting boyhood cronies. Maybe he was a guy who shouldn't have married. While he was talking, Kent, Inez, and Frank entered in rapid succession and took their usual places.

Frank said he was depressed. His son required surgery for an undescended testicle. Only twelve, the boy had already chalked up enough operations for a lifetime. Edna's laughter no longer annoyed him, Frank went on. He was now thinking about how he could help her. A woman he'd met at a cocktail party kept on calling him for dates, though he'd made it clear to her that he was married. But maybe his marriage was on the rocks anyway.

"Why don't you work out your feelings here?" Edna asked. "It would help your marriage if you concentrated on loving one of us."

Hortense seconded the suggestion. "I shouldn't ask you to stick to the straight and narrow for me, but it would help you to stay away from such a woman."

"But you women are weak and irresponsible," Kent asserted. "Inez showed she had guts when she came back to the group, but she's very unreliable. And why is she working so hard to set up alliances with Frank and me?"

"I've given up on you, but Frank sounds so lonely he breaks my heart," she said. "His sad voice makes me feel close to him."

Frank reacted quickly: "Thanks for the sympathy, but I think I can take care of things myself. I'm thinking about my son. That's why I'm depressed."

Edna was sorry she hadn't brought him a souvenir from Mexico, as she had for Hortense and Inez. "I'd better concentrate on why I didn't get anything for the men."

"You offered us the greatest gift of all and we all turned you down," Frank reminded her with some derision.

She offered herself, in Carter's opinion, to encourage the men to talk out feelings. Sexual satisfaction from each other would be a poor substitute for what they really wanted.

All kinds of gifts were needed, Edna commented. She described the pin and earrings in the two parcels she had brought in.

Interrupting her impatiently, Kent asked: "Don't you realize you're leading us into a mess of chitchat?"

"Why not? I'm talking about tokens of my affection. I'm leading this group to talk of love."

Hortense inquired if that was true. Then she asked me: "Why are you so quiet today?"

There was nothing I was ready to deal with at that moment, but I wanted to reply. "I've been thinking about the order in which you arrived today."

That was the first thought that had entered my mind during the session. The two women whom I knew longest had come in first. The sequence in which the others followed reflected the duration of their relationship with me and, perhaps, the intensity of their desire for my affection.

This statement was misinterpreted by the latecomers; they took it as a reproach. They volunteered explanations which made me aware that they felt guilty about canceling the last session. I studied their reactions but did not comment on them.

Kent had no enthusiasm about coming that afternoon. He couldn't understand why the women thought about the members of the group between sessions. He wanted to report two extraordinary dreams he'd had since the last meeting. The first was about a broken arm. A week later he dreamt that he had a cracked ankle and scoured the city in vain for a physician who would tend to it. No one paid any attention to him.

"He has a way of looking at people as if he's communicating with them when he really isn't," said Inez. "Kent, tell us why you never think of us outside this office."

"She's trying to get some feeling from you, Kent," Frank intervened. "Why are you so irritable?"

Kent denied that he was, and Frank and Edna argued the point with him. Inez put some gum into her mouth and said: "I feel lonely again."

"That's because he's rejecting you," Edna asserted. "You are asking for his penis."

Why did women always take things personally? Kent's voice reflected annoyance again. He could have warm feelings for people even if they irritated him.

"You're practically psychotic," Inez said angrily. "I know you think the same of me and I hope you hate me. My skin would crawl at the thought of being loved by a weakling like you. You remind me of my husband."

"Then I can understand his troubles with you. You try too hard to let him know you're alive."

"I think you're right, Kent," Carter spoke up. "My wife does the same thing. It's hard for me to take it. She objects to my leaving her when I have work to do. But I'm not certain what I really want from her."

"What are your thoughts about this, Dr. Spotnitz?" Edna looked bewildered.

"I'm interested in your complaints about being unloved," I said. "You don't feel loved by people who really love you. Kent's dreams demonstrate your feelings. He runs around looking for someone to take care of him. You all want to be loved, but don't do any loving. Why?"

"Where is it stuck, our love?" Hortense asked.

"But don't you want to be loved too?" Inez put the question to me.

What interested me was their feelings, I told her; that is, their feelings of being unloved and their need for feeling loved. Frank felt he needed love because his son faced an operation, Kent because he felt crippled, and Carter couldn't think of any reason. They all had some problem about getting the feeling of love they wanted.

"I'd like to love," Frank interrupted, "but I can't do it on demand."

Wearily, Kent asked: "Are we supposed to love unendingly?"

Inez wanted to apologize for what she had said to him. She would try to please him instead of demanding affection from him.

I asked her: "Why don't you feel you are entitled to some emotional responsiveness for yourself? This is another demonstration that chewing gum is a substitute for what you really want. You are defiantly acting out your resentment instead of expressing it in words." [1]

"He really is like my husband," Inez said. "Why do I always pick out a man who can't respond to me as I want?"

"You attach yourself to men who have the same need for affection that you do," I explained. "But then your demands on them make them feel more inadequate."

"That statement gives me great insight," Kent spoke animatedly. "Now I know why I always feel crippled when women say they love me. They demand love that I can't give them, so their request for it makes me feel even more defective. I want to crawl away from them because they make me feel even less like a man. My wife doesn't make such demands on me; that's why I stick with her."

"You are saying that she makes you feel more adequate," I pointed out. "All of you have some problem about love.

[1] This understanding and the emotional experience resolved her need to chew gum compulsively. Two weeks later Inez announced on her arrival that she felt much better and would not chew gum. This was her first voluntary statement to that effect.

You hunger for it but can't digest it. You don't assimilate anything now but understanding. That's the complexity of the situation."

"We've been busy feeling hatred," said Edna. "Maybe this blocked us from feeling love. But I must have felt love for two people here since I thought about them last week and bought gifts for them. I hope the love will last."

"You're supposed to talk about love here, not buy gifts," I said. "The love you feel for each other in these sessions is dissipated when you act on the feelings. It is important for you to feel and talk about love, become aware of how it develops and the reactions it induces in you when you are exposed to it. This group needs to discuss this further and increase its understanding of feelings of love and their effects." I arose from my chair to indicate that the session was over. "Have a good week."

As I rearranged the room after their departure, I thought about how the problem of giving love had coincided with the problem of getting it, enabling me to work simultaneously on the resistances to verbalizing love and aggression. I also thought about how I had let myself be shut out of the discussion until the last ten or fifteen minutes. True, I did not talk as much as I had thought I might. That was because the group members functioned well without me, tackling on their own initiative the very problems that I had decided to start working on with them that afternoon.

Was it simply a coincidence that they felt the significant feelings I had been thinking about and were learning how to express them? It was also within the realm of possibility that telepathic communication was going on during the session between my patients and myself. In psychotherapy as in other human contacts, messages appear at times to be transmitted from one mind to another in other ways than through the senses. My patients often tell me that I take their thoughts "right out of" their heads. It is generally agreed that intuition figures prominently in the treatment process, but whether our "hunches" are based only on sensory impressions or may also involve extrasensory perceptions, such as mental telepathy, is a much-debated topic.

For many years I have assumed that telepathic processes do operate in psychotherapy; but I no longer attempt to prove the validity of the assumption. When patients share it, as they often do, and question me about it, I accept the possibility and let it rest at that. Generally, they seem to respond more effectively to treatment when I take it for granted that telepathic communication may be going on in the course of a session. However, I prefer to leave the investigation of these phenomena to observers who are directly concerned with evaluating them, because it has been my experience that preoccupation with such occurrences interferes with therapy. Regardless of whether the "meeting of minds" I had been aware of during that group session was coincidental or telepathic, it sounded a pleasant note in my afterthoughts on the session.

The interchanges and speculations of that afternoon represent a sampling of one analyst's activity with individuals and groups in the course of his practice. His words and attitudes, though highly diverse, spring from the same analytic data: his patients' behavior, thoughts, feelings, and memories, and his own. He translates his observations of the unknown or incomprehensible into understandable language. He invests the fund of his emotions in communications that will neutralize harmful life experiences and help people produce, in healthful ways, the chemistry of love and hate.

[7]

"Whatsoever I Shall See or Hear"

"ONE OF MY group members is flirting with crime, and I've been feeling like his accomplice ever since I found out about it."

A fleeting vision of a woman with the face of a Fra Angelico angel peering through prison bars made me smile, but Amy White, as I shall call her, spoke in utter sincerity. She is a young clinical psychologist who consults me regularly about problems which arise in her group-therapy practice. Usually we discuss the total significance of disclosures made in her group sessions. But during the consultation of which I write, she was concerned about some information being withheld from a group.

Nicholas had told it to her privately, after absenting himself from the last session of the group. It was a new one he had joined after more than a year of individual psychotherapy. He had entered it in a state of depression.

After doing well in individual treatment with Miss White and making a good start in the group, he had become depressed and uncommunicative. When other members asked if something was troubling him, he denied it; but their expressions of concern seemed to make him more anxious. Then he had arranged to see her alone. Our consultation took place shortly after that meeting.

Nicholas was a man in his thirties, a procurement officer for an official agency, his therapist told me. He had an ailing wife and three small children to support on a modest salary. Though they lived frugally, he had gone heavily in debt to provide his wife with the best medical treatment available. When he himself became depressed and worn down by his worries, he was advised to enter psychotherapy. His widowed mother had agreed to pay for his treatment. She was a highly religious woman who took pride in her son's honorable record as a civil servant.

A representative of a new manufacturing concern bidding for a contract from Nicholas's agency had proposed making the award "well worth his while," he told Miss White privately. The "handsome" consideration secretly offered him would pay off many of his debts. The concern probably merited the award, he asserted; besides, what he contemplated doing was done "every day," judging by some of his colleagues' veiled allusions to his holier-than-thou attitude. Nicholas was known as a man who never accepted a rake-off. He had always frowned at the corrupt practices they hinted at; but he was impressed with how well they provided for their families. And they never seemed to get into any trouble.

Nevertheless, it was a risky situation. He feared he would be disgraced and end up in prison if he assented to the deal and the facts ever came out. He could get in trouble by talking about this in the group; yet he felt guilty about not talking about it. Wasn't he required to say everything that occurred to him? Did Miss White agree with him that he should conceal this information from the group?

"Did you find out why he is putting you in the position of making you an accessory before the fact?" I asked her. "He may be trying to find out how corruptible you are."

That was possible, but she doubted that the man was aware of it. They had developed a fairly good relationship in the course of his individual treatment. He seemed confident that he could tell her anything without getting into trouble. Besides, he hadn't done anything corrupt yet; he had come to her primarily to explain why he was behaving so strangely in the group.

"I was so horrified to hear what he considered doing that I had a strong urge to implore him not to do it," she went on. "I realize now why I was so tempted to be motherly with him, instead of behaving like an analyst. I would be shocked to learn that any patient of mine was involved in some shady business, but Nicholas especially. He has been such an upright person. Early in treatment he professed great esteem for high moral standards, and I know he meant it. He said he would never enjoy anything in life that he could not come by honorably."

How did she account for the change in him?

"After he began to 'unwind,' he got to realize that he really resented the emotional price of denying himself and his family the opportunity to live better. He now feels that his debts, his frugality, and his failure to give his family a few luxuries all contributed to his depression. These feelings make him very vulnerable to temptation. I'm glad I warned him not to take any important decisions before discussing them with me."

She had responded objectively to Nicholas's disclosure, Miss White continued. After listening to him quietly, she had suggested that he think some more about the matter and discuss it with her again before attending another group session. Meanwhile, she was undecided what to do. What alternatives lay before her?

If she did not want to work with Nicholas further, I assured her that she would be justified in discharging him from treatment. Either one of them had the right to break off their relationship at any time. Some analysts issue a warning to this effect. That is, if a patient reveals that he is engaging in some questionable activity or intends to engage in it, they tell him: If you go on with this, I will stop treating you.

"Is that your approach?" she asked.

"Very rarely. Instead of trying to influence a patient by threats, I prefer to make him aware of the possible consequences of his anti-social behavior, or the adverse effects it would have on his treatment. Once I have put him in full possession of the facts, I step aside and let him make his own decision. I help him halt or delay engaging in the questionable conduct, if possible, until he understands his impulse to engage in it. With these alternatives in mind, how would you prefer to proceed with this man? Do you want to discharge him now that he is on the verge of doing something crooked?"

"Oh, no," she replied. "At least not at present. I have a lot of feeling for him, and I want to help him get over his depression. Wouldn't I be punishing him worse than society would if I discharged him because he told me what he is tempted to do? Once I got over the shock, I practically made up my mind to this. But I have other questions. First of all, I want to reassure myself on one point. It's pretty clear in my mind that I am not required by law to report what Nicholas tells me."

"Why is that clear to you?"

"Under the code of my profession, the disclosures made to me in treatment sessions are privileged communications," she replied. "Besides, I'm treating this man under psychiatric supervision, so in a sense I'm doubly privileged. What I'm really uncertain about, though, is how he should be handled in the group. It's only a few months old. I don't know some of the members well enough to predict how they would react if he began talking about what he told me. They understand they're not supposed to divulge what goes on in the sessions; but I pride myself on being too good a psychologist to try to force them to react the way I want them to. I suspect that one of the women would feel it was her duty to inform on anyone who talked about being involved in something criminal."

"Would you encourage him to talk about it in the group?"

"Certainly not," she said. "He's told me that he's afraid to talk about it. But I can't be sure that his strong guilt feelings won't force him to blurt out everything. He already feels like a crook. And if he becomes one, he'd be all the more tempted to use the group as a confessional."

Since he was aware of the danger, why did she think he would do that?

"To satisfy the great need he'd have for punishment," Miss White answered. "And he might succeed in getting himself punished."

"Why would you be more interested in protecting him from this than he is in protecting himself?"

The question startled Miss White. It hadn't occurred to her, she said, that she had been trying to "protect him from himself." The very fact that I could ask her this was a clue that she was becoming more involved with Nicholas than she would like to be. Nevertheless, ought she to discourage him from giving any of this information to the group?

I asked her why she thought this would be advisable.

"To let him know I agree with him that it would be undesirable to talk about it," she replied. "Confirming his fears might make it less likely that he'd use the group rule to punish himself. Abuse it, I should say. Oh, of course, I could peg the whole discussion with him to the group rule. I have to help him understand his conflict about talking about himself."

"Do you still think it would be advisable to discourage him from talking?"

"I see what you mean," she asserted. "Of course not. You've helped me realize that I was in danger of getting involved in this dirty business myself. He's been relying on the group rule to justify his need to expose himself and get punished, and I was tempted to respond directly to that need and tell him what to do. I know now how I want to handle him."

A few weeks later, Miss White gave me an account of her discussion with Nicholas. "I started out by asking him why he thought he should tell the group about the rake-off offered him. He was just trying to obey the rule to talk about everything, he said. Why was there such a rule? Well, since this was a therapy group, he assumed that the purpose of the rule was to help the members get well. My next question was this: How will your talking about this matter help you and the other members of your group get well? We talked about that for a while. He couldn't see how this disclosure would be helpful to the others; but he thought their reactions might help him, maybe help him make up his mind about taking the rake-off. But finally he decided that discussing the matter wouldn't be helpful to any of them.

"Then I asked if he thought it would be harmful to discuss it. He made short shrift of that question. The disclosure would probably be very disturbing to the other members, and would leave him wide open to exposure. If the facts became known, he could lose his job even if he turned down the bribe."

Miss White told Nicholas that she agreed with him. Talking about this matter would not be helpful, and it was realistic to assume that it could be harmful. Then he stated: "I understand. You're telling me not to bring it up."

"I reminded him again that I had no intention of telling him what to do," Miss White continued. "He would have to decide that for himself. Thus far, we had been considering whether the disclosure would improve his emotional health and that of the other group members. We had agreed that most likely it would not be helpful. But that might not be what he wanted to accomplish anyway. I suggested that we next investigate his motives. Was he thinking of stealing and talking about stealing because he wanted to harm himself and the other group members?"

At this point Nicholas interrupted her. "You're right," he said. "I have no business talking about this in the group. Obviously, the others would tell me not to take the rake-off; maybe I was tempted to talk because I wanted them to frighten me into not taking it. The only thing I could accomplish would be to get myself punished if I take it. I don't know them well enough to be sure they wouldn't get me into trouble. I won't discuss it."

"Nicholas is behaving very well in the group now," Amy White continued. "He's begun to talk about his family life, and said something about his war experiences. He's made some thoughtful comments about matters raised by other group members. But nary a word about the rake-off. By the way, he told me he hadn't yet made up his mind what to do about it. I suggested that he make himself fully aware of what he was doing and why before he did anything. I'm pleased about the way I handled the treatment situation, but I'd like to think I also helped him make the right decision. Do you think I'll ever know if he took that bribe?"

"Why are you so eager to know?"

She smiled. "I see I'm getting too involved again. I'll just deal with whatever he brings up for discussion."

For more than a year, I heard nothing more about this problem. The next time Miss White mentioned it, she was in high spirits.

"Here's a postscript on Nicholas," she started out. "He's getting over his depression, and he's on very good terms with the other group members. They know now why he acted so strangely for a while at the beginning. He talked about it in a rather wonderful way at the last session."

"You sound happy," I commented. "Did virtue triumph?"

"Let me tell you how he explained it," she said. "A woman in the group talked about being shocked by the TV quiz scandal. One of the men accused her of being very naïve. He quoted George Bernard Shaw's remark about honesty varying with the strain put on it. Nicholas said he disagreed, though he himself was sorely tempted, not long ago, to take the same cynical attitude. His treatment had helped him find an honorable solution to his problems, and he felt like talking about it.

"He'd had opportunities in his work to get money in underhanded ways, he went on, but the only time he was in real danger of besmirching his record was shortly after he entered the group. He was greatly tempted then to take a rake-off on a contract. This seemed to be the only way he could get the money he needed, because his job didn't pay him enough to meet his family expenses and bring up his children the way he wanted to. If he hadn't been afraid of ending up in prison, he might have given in. Later on, when they exchanged ideas about their problems and feelings of inadequacy, he said, he got to realize that he had a serious shortcoming: lack of initiative.

"Nicholas told the group that for several months he'd been asking himself: Hasn't the job which has opened up opportunities to get money illegitimately also given me the experience to get more money legitimately? The idea gave him fresh confidence in his own ability, he said. He's been looking about for a better-paying job. One has just come through; he's going to join a firm of management consultants at a much higher salary. Nicholas was cheerful about leaving his old post with a spotless record. He said it was a great relief to him to know that he had sowed all of his wild oats in his mind."

After this statement, his co-members congratulated him. One of them expressed pleasure that he had found them helpful.

"At that point, I wondered if I would get a posy too," Miss White continued. "But what do you think happened? Nicholas told the others about coming to me when he was grappling with his conflict. He complained about my attitude. Instead of telling him what to do about the rake-off, I'd asked him a lot of questions and forced him to think out the whole thing himself. It was very aggravating. He might have come to the wrong conclusion because I'd made him stand on his own two feet."

Ethical problems like those which confronted Amy White in this case are raised by other psychotherapists who consult me, and arise in my own practice. Analytic psycho-therapy is unique in its "emphasis on the daemonic in nature, its passion for investigating the night-side of the soul," [1] as Thomas Mann has observed. The road to recovery is paved with verbalizations of potentially dangerous, even explosive forces: emotional drives which fight the control of reason and threaten to erupt into destructive behavior. In some cases they have already erupted. Conduct sympto-matic of emotional disturbances makes some patients vul-nerable to social ostracism or even to criminal prosecution.

The practitioner who treats them has to resolve conflicts between his professional obligations and his responsibilities as a citizen to uphold the social mores and co-operate with the constituted legal authorities. In putting the welfare of the patient above all other considerations, he may appear to be failing in his civic duties. Should he continue to treat someone who has engaged in reprehensible behavior or has incipient tendencies to do so? How should he respond to disclosures of perverse acts surrounded by powerful social taboos? These are issues involving proper regard for the patient, his family, and society which have to be reconciled on the basis of personal judgment.

To me many of these conflicts seem more apparent than real. If I temporarily renounce my social obligations, I do so to help a patient ultimately outgrow his anti-social tendencies and function more creditably in the community. Retaliatory punishment for past transgressions won't cure

[1] In *Past Masters*, translated by H. T. Lowe-Porter (New York: Alfred A. Knopf; 1933), p. 191.

the offender of these tendencies; often it damages him. His emotional disorder cannot be treated on the basis of moral judgments. To motivate him to give up his offensive conduct and help him become the kind of person he would like to be, I give him learning experiences—emotional training.

In the course of this training, he may make disclosures about actionable conduct. I exercise my legal privilege to respect the privacy of his communications. In doing this, I also uphold that well-known stipulation of the Oath of Hippocrates never to divulge "whatsoever I shall see or hear in the course of my profession, as well as outside my profession in my intercourse with men, if it be what should not be published abroad."

As a medical student, I was impressed with the value of confidentiality in the doctor-patient relationship. The importance of this principle was repeatedly borne out by my experiences as an intern and resident in general and psychiatric hospitals. Some patients, I observed, were pained by any intrusion on their privacy, such as having their bodies uncovered for examination. To be gossiped about by nurses or other attendants or to have their medical charts dangle the particulars of their illness before any curious stranger greatly upset them. Anticipating an unfavorable reaction to complaints, they usually nursed their anger in silence. This is not healthful. The privacy of some of our feelings deserves to be respected but buried resentments are not among them. They tend to create, conceal, or preserve mental illness.

In the treatment of bodily ailments, confidentiality is incidental to the curative processes and, by and large, has little direct bearing on a patient's recovery. If he is in psychological treatment, confidentiality is of far greater significance. Self-revelation is an integral part of the psychotherapeutic process. Knowledge that the privacy of his disclosures is respected greatly facilitates his recovery.

The physician's first job is not to harm his patient. His second is to help him, if possible. It is not helpful, and is usually detrimental for a person, to feel that he might get punished for what he has to reveal about himself in psychotherapy. Even in the intimacy of a favorably developing one-to-one relationship, he often anticipates being harmed by some disclosure. "Do I really have to talk about this?" I hear him say. He has to be educated to the fact that I am trustworthy, and why.

In certain respects, the principle of confidentiality has to be applied more flexibly in the treatment of emotional disorders than in general medicine. In psychiatric practice, the need to protect a seriously disturbed patient from endangering his own life or the lives of others arises from time to time. In such an emergency, it naturally becomes more important to prevent him from committing an act of violence than to respect his confidence. Some practitioners inform a patient's family if they believe that he has homicidal or suicidal tendencies. This is sometimes done without his consent.

I have never had to do this. Early in my practice, if I thought there was any danger that a man who talked about killing his wife, for example, would actually do so, I would suggest that he send her in to talk to me or permit me to telephone her and warn her that she was in danger. If you're going to do violence and end up in prison, I would tell the man, what's the point of continuing our relationship? The threat of being discharged from treatment usually served as a sobering deterrent; in a few cases, the patient was admitted to a mental hospital.

The successes and failures resulting from this tactical

approach helped me to devise a more certain barrier against destructive behavior—the verbalization of the patient's aggressive impulses as early as possible in treatment. When one focuses on securing the release of these impulses in language from the opening session, any tendencies to do violence usually get "talked out" within six months. Warnings to the family, with or without a patient's consent, therefore become unnecessary.

As a beginning analyst, I followed the general practice of sharing with a trusted consultant some of the disclosures made by a patient. Though his identity was always concealed, he did not know about this "control work" while it was going on. This gave me some qualms of conscience, but they had to be endured. Knowledge that I was disclosing some information meant for my ears alone would have been harmful to the patient while he was in the throes of acute conflict. After this was resolved, perhaps a year or two later, I could inform him about the consultations without causing distress. He would usually express pleasure at the thought that I considered him so important or his case so interesting that I had consulted a colleague about him. Similarly, in my own practice, psychotherapists who consult me entrust me with information divulged to them by their own patients.

In individual treatment, however, breaches of confidence are relatively circumspect and unavoidable. They involve a similarly privileged colleague or, in a more extreme case involving physical safety, the patient's immediate family. By comparison, group treatment appears to violate the spirit as well as the letter of the principle of confidentiality. Some believe that it represents a deliberate overthrow of the principle.

Undeniably, the ethical problems of the psychotherapist

take on new dimensions when he treats patients in groups. Issues of personal conscience are not the only ones which confront him. He has to gamble to some extent on his ability to protect his group members from being harmed by gossip or malicious disclosure of any facts they reveal in their treatment sessions. He has to anticipate their reactions to various types of disclosures, and resolve any obstacles to their functioning as assistant therapists to each other.

Will it be safe, the psychotherapist may ask himself, for a group member to talk about some actionable type of behavior in the presence of other persons suffering from emotional disturbance and, in any event, not legally privileged to respect his confidence? Will it, moreover, be desirable for them to hear what he has to say, or will it interfere with their own progress? In the group therapist's judgment, to put it briefly: Will it be possible for him to maintain enough confidentiality in the group to safeguard its members from harm and help them get well?

These questions suggest the risks inherent in co-operative treatment. They suggest, too, why some practitioners lack enthusiasm for it. Having been educated to the idea that confidentiality requires an absolutely private relationship with a patient, they find the idea of sharing his communications with other patients distasteful, if not repugnant.

I must confess that it took me a long time to conquer my own initial aversion to the idea. I was not an advocate of privacy for its own sake; but I doubted that a climate conducive to emotional growth could be created without it. Strangers meeting together to engage in self-revelation, it seemed to me, would fight to preserve the privacy of their illness, notably, by burying their resentment over having to share time and attention and listen to each other's disclosures. If they did not release these feelings in language during the sessions, they would be unable to develop the understanding and profound feelings of love that lead to mental health.

My doubts were not fully dispelled until I found out how to resolve the obstacles to the verbal expression of negative feelings in the group and, in this way, to create a climate of confidentiality for its members. It develops, experience has taught me, when patients seated together in a small circle go on talking hour after hour about their true feelings, neither withdrawing nor coming to blows over the most hateful things they say to each other. The atmosphere of mutual trust and acceptance which comes into being when they operate in this way can be utilized to produce basic personality change.

After exploring various approaches and precautionary measures employed in the field, I came to the conclusion that the way to create a climate of group confidentiality is to resolve the obstacles to it in the natural course of treatment. By dealing with tendencies to violate the secrecy of group disclosures as special forms of resistance to co-operative functioning, I find it possible to train group members to respond appropriately to any kind of disclosures that have to be made. This training process permits them to evolve into relatedness instead of having it forced upon them. Problems involving confidentiality have practically dropped out of my practice since I adopted this approach.

Before then, I thought a great deal about the possibility that a patient might divulge some information that would get him into trouble. I investigated the safeguards commonly introduced to protect the privacy of group communications. A few of these seem desirable and necessary. Others I rejected as not consonant with my own approach.

Some psychotherapists extract an oath or pledge of secrecy from members of their groups. Any one who is unable to keep his word may then be weeded out of the group. For the therapist who does not wish to work with such a person, it is advantageous to have this option to discharge him.

One of my objections to swearing patients to secrecy is that it puts a strain on the treatment relationship. Some are either incapable of keeping their word when they enter a group or would be exposed to undesirable stress if they were asked for an oath or pledge. If patients are able to control their behavior in my office, I am willing to train them to carry out requirements which they cannot meet willingly and easily when they begin their treatment. Educating them to keep their word when they give it, and not to give it when they cannot keep it, are both aspects of their training to function more effectively in life.

The introduction of a swearing-in ritual seems undesirable to me for other reasons. The group operates for purposes of therapy, not as a secret society. Demands made on patients for special commitments are apt to give them the impression that they are engaged in some underhanded procedure or are flaunting society in some way.

There is no negative in man's unconscious. Telling him not to do something implants the idea of doing it, perhaps irresistibly so if he is negatively suggestible. That is another objection to pledging members not to betray group confidences. Even without the pledge, too much stress on the rule of confidentiality at the start of treatment may stimulate group members to violate it. I find it more salutary to ask how they feel about keeping things confidential and to help them explore their own attitudes on the subject. A person who glibly asserts that "of course" he would never divulge what went on in the group may be asked if he believes in keeping secrets from the public. As tendencies to comply blindly with the rule or to violate it are investigated, members get to understand why privacy of communication is desirable.

One important safeguard is built into the treatment process. It does not require that the group member disclose his name, address, place of employment, or any other biographical data. In some special groups, whose members' sexually aberrant behavior makes them vulnerable to prosecution, badges with fictitious names are worn during the sessions. Members of my groups address each other by their first names—the standard procedure in most privately conducted groups. As group members get to know and trust each other, they usually drop many clues to their actual identity; but in principle they can function throughout treatment as complete strangers. In the future I plan to dispense with even first-name introductions when a new group gets under way; the members will be permitted to identify themselves in any way they please.

The policy of assembling strangers for a group and encouraging them to remain so is one that I follow as consistently as possible. As a private practitioner whose groups are composed primarily of persons he has treated individually, I make exceptions to this policy from time to time. Some persons who are professional acquaintances either ask me to treat them together or do not object to each other's presence in the treatment sessions. Thus far I have been spared the plight of the therapist practicing in a small community who finds himself introducing social acquaintances or neighbors at the first group session. One way of coping with this eventuality is to permit patients to rotate among several groups before assigning them to one on a regular basis.

Apart from the fact that most persons prefer to be treated with strangers and are less inhibited in their presence, this policy fosters confidentiality in other ways. If two or more members are acquainted when the group starts to function, or have outside associations during the course of treatment, their progress in treatment is apt to be uneven. Their social ties encourage the formation of sub-groups. These introduce crosscurrents into the sessions, feelings of separate intimacy which tend to dispel or impede the development of total group intimacy.

At the beginning of my group practice, I considered it to be undesirable for patients to subject their communications to any form of self-censorship. The fundamental rule of psychoanalytic treatment—free association, or telling everything that comes to one's mind—would obviously lead to bedlam if one tried to apply it strictly in a group situation. However, it was then my opinion that the analytic process would be adversely affected if the members of a group did not function in the spirit of free association; that is, talk spontaneously about whatever came to mind to the extent possible in co-operative treatment. Consequently, group members were told that the withholding of any information about themselves constituted unco-operative behavior.

Some of them, especially overimpulsive persons, responded too literally to the instruction to "tell everything." It was impossible to predict the kind of disclosures they would make; some made statements which were received with expressions of strong disapproval or horror. These intensely negative reactions were undesirable. They interfered with the even development of the members' feelings for each other and stimulated impulses to divulge information to outsiders.

In the initial phase of her group treatment, for example, one young woman said she hesitated to apply for a government position for which she was highly qualified. As a college student, she continued, she had belonged to an organization which the Attorney General later listed as subversive. She feared that she might therefore be debarred from federal employment or harassed if she submitted an application.

"Don't you dare, or you'll regret it." The warning came from another woman in the group. "I'll report you to the FBI."

The speaker did not carry out her threat, but she meant it at the time. It infected the group with the spirit of the witch hunt for some time. There were references to the "informer in our midst."

In another new group, a very excitable man talked about an argument he had been embroiled in with his wife. He asserted: "She makes me so mad I could kill her." A woman who felt threatened by the statement said she intended to find out his name and address and report him to the police.

"Why are you trying to protect his wife?" I intervened. "Have you forgotten that you're a member of a therapy group? All you have to do is convince him to go to a mental hospital if he's sick enough to behave that way."

The irate husband growled: "Can't I say what I feel without being taken so seriously?"

These episodes did not create substantial damage, but, like a charge of dynamite set off without advance warning or precautions, they could have done so. Instructing the patient entering a group to talk about everything is, as a matter of fact, like playing with dynamite. It may produce explosions which will interfere with the group's forward movement. Unless its members have been conditioned to respond properly to information which stirs up intense feelings, these disclosures are not invariably therapeutic.

"Tell the story of your life," the instruction I now give my groups, initiates self-revelation more equably. This modification of the rule of free-association developed out of my experience in individual psychotherapy. I had observed that the instruction to free-associate tended to aggravate the difficulty of forming good relationships with persons suffering from severe disorders. Often they felt that they would "go crazy" if they told "everything"; this requirement intensified their panic and hopelessness about getting well. Such a patient has less difficulty in starting to talk, I found, if I issued an invitation to this effect: Tell the story of your life in any way you wish, and I'll study how you do it. Since everyone undergoing psychoanalytic therapy eventually tells the story of his life naturally and spontaneously through his behavior, feelings, and words, the patient was just being invited to do what he was bound to do.

This approach reassured him; even if he could not talk in an emotionally significant way at first, he felt that he was co-operating if he talked about what he had done the day before, his lunch, or some other non-threatening subject. Meanwhile, he was being slowly educated to meet the demands of free association. The patterns of his communication proved to be of great significance in understanding him. Since my experience with these difficult cases indicated that unnecessary stagnation could be eliminated at the beginning of psychotherapy through this approach, I now employ it generally in my practice.

In group treatment the life-story concept has an additional value; it facilitates confidentiality. The group member experiences no pressure to "spill out everything at once" when he is acting on the instruction to tell the story of his life. When he listens, on the other hand, he is not apt to be confronted with startling disclosures so suddenly that he gets to feel like a medical student on his first visit to the autopsy room. Consequently, the raw recruits from the outside community are not bludgeoned into a suspension of moral judgments, social conventions, and their individual biases. Given time to become psychologically intimate, they gradually acquire some awareness of each other's motives and customary behavior. They also undergo a desensitizing process which enables them to serve as "loving healers" and to operate spontaneously in the spirit of medical privacy.

An atmosphere of reserve is fostered for at least a year, which generally covers the first third of the treatment process. Group members are encouraged to engage in self-revelation in slow stages and at about the same pace. They are helped to test out the group climate until they feel sufficiently secure, internally and externally, to discuss any subject. Threats or fears of exposure are responded to in the same way as other obstacles to communication.

If a patient comes to me privately and expresses misgivings about divulging some fact about himself, we review the possibility that he would be harmed by any leakage of the information. We also consider whether the disclosure would be too upsetting to his co-patients at that time. If we agree that the information should be withheld for a while, the questionable subject may be "talked around" intermittently for many sessions before the disclosure is made. If absolutely necessary, a problem can be handled in individual sessions, but I prefer to have it brought up, sooner or later, for discussion in the group.

Timing, not exclusion, is the essence of this approach.

After a climate of confidentiality has been created, group members are generally capable of responding in a therapeutic way to all of the disclosures that have to be made in treatment sessions. Then it seems natural to them to scientifically investigate behavior which would be unmentionable elsewhere.

In a training course which I conducted a few years ago, a young psychiatrist entering group practice solicited advice about the handling of a sensitive disclosure in a group which had just started to function. Jerome, one of its members, remained after a session to ask the psychiatrist if there wasn't some limit to the "everything" that group members were supposed to reveal about themselves. The young man went on: "What I'm trying to find out is this: Do you really want me to talk about committing incest with my sister?"

Was he referring to some experience of childhood, he was asked. Such revelations are usually accepted with equanimity; sometimes they stimulate fantasies or other helpful memories.

"I don't mind talking about things I did as a kid," Jerome replied. "But this happened just two years ago, and how do I know it might not happen again? We sort of drifted into it, and I'm too ashamed to talk about it before these people. Wouldn't they throw me out of the group, or even report me?"

I asked the other therapists attending the seminar how they would handle such a situation in their own group practice. The animated discussion which followed reflected the various opinions and approaches in the field.

Persons who have committed any kind of illegal act don't belong in a general group conducted by a private practitioner. That was the opinion of several members of the seminar. After their attention was called to the wide range of actionable conduct, two of them reconsidered; they would also take into account the nature of the crime committed. One woman advocated excluding or dropping from a group any patient whose disclosures would arouse a great deal of horror or revulsion in other members. She would accept a kleptomaniac or homosexual, she went on, but not someone whose disclosures would concern incest as an adult or some other act hedged around by powerful social taboos.

The majority of those present favored a more liberal approach. One stated that he was guided to some extent by his attitudes about the law which the doubtful candidate had transgressed. He evaluated each case on an individual basis, he added, but he regarded the laws dealing with homosexuality and incest as antiquated. Some of the therapists attending the seminar indicated that they instructed members of their groups to withhold unduly sensitive information from their co-patients. Such communications were dealt with only in individual sessions.

The young man whose question was the basis for this discussion was not withdrawn from group treatment nor was mention of the subject about which he had given warning foreclosed throughout the group's existence. His psychotherapist decided to adopt my own approach.

Jerome's misgivings were discussed with him privately. He was asked: "Don't you think it might be detrimental to you and the others for the time being to talk about your relationship with your sister? If there's no great urgency about discussing it, why not bide your time until you think that it's safe for you to talk about it?"

"I certainly would prefer that," Jerome replied, "but

won't that interfere with my treatment? I thought the rule was that I talk about everything."

"Does the rule require you to tell everything to everybody immediately?"

For many months the therapist took "soundings" of the group attitudes. In an opportune moment he reminded the members that they were supposed to talk freely about themselves during the sessions. "But how would you people feel," he inquired, "if someone here started to talk about being involved in some illegal activity?"

She wouldn't remain in a group which talked about anything illegal, one woman declared. She might be tempted to tip off the authorities.

"This is a group where we are supposed to get better by talking about anything that bothers us," a man reproved her. "Didn't you agree to keep things confidential when we started?"

Another man stated that he couldn't say in advance how he would react. It would depend on what was disclosed.

This opened a leisurely probe of their attitudes about specific anti-social acts. How would they feel about discussing stealing or fire-setting? An illicit office romance? Homosexuality? Perjury? Incest? At first mention of each act, the members expressed horror or revulsion at the thought of discussing it. As the discussion continued, however, one of them would recall a situation in which he had been tempted to behave in the same way. Similar admissions usually followed. The recognition that they had all had impulses to commit the same acts at some time in their lives desensitized them further. Eventually, the attitude that they could deal with any information revealed and keep it confidential gained general acceptance.

After a while, the probe became somewhat academic. Before it ended, three group members had implicated themselves in anti-social behavior. A woman who complained about her unhappy love life volunteered the information that she had undergone an illegal abortion. Another talked about flitting from one homosexual relationship to another. A man branded himself as a "wife thief." He had "stolen" a woman from her husband and then deserted her, he said, because they were unhappy together. He feared that he was on the verge of repeating the pattern.

Jerome did not consult his group therapist privately again before he started to talk about his relationship with his sister. When he sensed that the group could accept the information, he made the disclosure, painfully but with considerable composure. After he had finished what he wanted to say, the woman who had talked about her abortion broke the momentary silence. She murmured: "And I thought I was the worst criminal here." Other group members expressed shock or revulsion.

In later sessions they demonstrated that they had dealt successfully with these reactions. When Jerome talked about his incestuous wishes, they helped him to understand and resolve his emotional disturbance. It was one of many problems which were investigated in a non-judgmental way during the group experience.

Through the approach just illustrated, I have found that any kind of difficulty which has to be brought up can usually be divulged to group members without precipitating undesirable reactions. Eventually, they find it possible to say anything they want to in their sessions, secure in the knowledge that their disclosures will not harm them. They develop feelings of loyalty, friendship, even a sense of responsibility about helping each other. When the group gets to have a real meaning for them, they respect each other's confidence not only because this is expected of them; it is also the way they want to operate.

Even though most patients feel free to talk about any subject when they are alone with me, they are not encouraged to start off with their most intimate disclosures. Early in my practice, I used to feel hurt if they asked if I would divulge any information they disclosed to me privately. Now I accept whatever attitudes they express about my trustworthiness as a subject for research. An investigation of my reliability serves as an object lesson for a person who is overly inclined to take the phantom figure too much for granted.

I asked one man who had been duped repeatedly because of his blind reliance on the word of strangers how he knew he wouldn't get into hot water again by talking with me. "How do you know I don't have a recorder under my couch and a loud-speaker hooked up in Times Square blaring out everything you say?" Laughing, he said that was the craziest thing he'd ever heard. He didn't know why, but I just wouldn't go "that far." In that case, how far would I go? Was the loud-speaker set up in his home? In Central Park? In my waiting-room? We followed wherever his fancy took it. Eventually, he got to know me as a real person, and to understand how much confidence to place in me. By that time we were both glad to forget about the loud-speaker.

It is usually much easier to conduct such an investigation in a group, since members are inclined to nurse fears at the start that one or more of their co-patients will betray their confidence. As these worries evaporate, they talk with increasing spontaneity about their current thoughts, feelings, and memories. Some find it more important to respect each other's confidences than those of their own spouses. I have observed that the psychological climate of a therapy group frequently gets to be more intimate than the marital climate.

My group members have never betrayed the trust I place in them as assistant therapists. Amazingly few serious violations of confidence have been reported by other group psychotherapists. One I heard about some years ago involved a divorce proceeding in which one group member, appearing as a witness for one of the parties, divulged information given by the other party during treatment. Would legislation to protect group members against such leakages be in order? This is a question which has recently been argued by psychotherapists who advocate a code of ethics governing group practice. The enlightened judge, in my opinion, would rule out such testimony as privileged communication.

Another violation was reported by Dr. Raymond H. Corsini [2] after more than a decade of personal experience in the group treatment of inmates of numerous prisons. In only one case did incriminating information divulged in a therapy session go further. It was reported by the guilty party himself.

With proper leadership and co-operative functioning, the therapy group tends to evolve into a therapeutic community which is hermetically sealed by the psychological kinship of its members. They cease to judge and condemn as they get to understand each other. The "black souls" emerge as human beings whose past aberrations are explanations for the present and lessons for the future.

[2] In: *Methods of Group Psychotherapy* (New York: McGraw-Hill Book Company, Inc., 1957), p. 128.

[8]

The Meaning of Recovery

I HAD A long telephone conversation one evening with a friend of mine, himself a physician, about the health of his sister-in-law. Since the death of her brother the previous week she had been having severe vomiting attacks; the first had taken place in the midst of the funeral services. She was confined to bed and had been examined by the family physician and several specialists. They had recommended numerous drugs, including anesthetics, and other medical measures; but she had not responded to any of them. The situation was desperate. My friend felt that psychiatric attention might be helpful. He asked me, at the behest of the patient's husband, if I could come to their home that evening to see her.

Since that would have been extremely difficult, I asked him if he thought the visit could be put off until the following evening.

"I guess that will do," he answered. "After all, this has been going on for a whole week, so I suppose she'll be able to take it for another day. But it's a dangerous situation and I would like you to see her."

When I arrived at the patient's home the next evening, my friend was there to greet me. However, the atmosphere was decidedly different from what I had expected. He escorted me to the living-room where I found several men and women engaged in conversation. One of them, seated in a relaxed manner on the sofa, was a poised and smartly dressed woman. She was introduced to me as Ruth, my patient.

"We have a surprise for you," said my friend. "As soon as we told Ruth that a psychiatrist was coming here to see her, she stopped vomiting. She hasn't had an attack in twenty-four hours. But don't ask me why I didn't cancel the visit. We are all so delighted we wanted you to come anyway. You ought to see for yourself how you cured her by agreeing to come here. You certainly earned this fee!"

During the *pro forma* consultation which followed in the patient's bedroom, she informed me that she had vomited frequently during her early childhood. She also disclosed that when she began vomiting again after her brother's death, she had despaired of ever being able to stop.

"But I stopped, and stopped for good, as soon as I heard that you were coming," she went on. "Now I feel fine, so there's really nothing to talk about. I've always had a deathly fear of psychiatrists."

As I rose to leave, I suggested that she might come to my office if she decided later that she wanted to talk to me further.

"Don't worry," she answered with absolute finality. "I'll never need you."

Apparently, Ruth knew what she was talking about. In the eight years which have elapsed since I made that visit, my physician friend has assured me, his sister-in-law has suffered no recurrence of the vomiting.

Fear of me may have induced other patients to put off seeing me, but this was the only case in which I effected a "cure" before seeing the patient. This is enough to deflate the ego of any psychiatrist.

It is almost as disconcerting to discover that practically all a patient needs is to be permitted to talk. To do nothing but listen quietly throughout a treatment session is what some of my colleagues call "baby-sitting." It is especially repugnant to any relatively inexperienced analyst who feels a strong need to demonstrate, through his interpretations, that he is worthy of his fee. Nevertheless, from time to time I have a patient whose recovery depends upon the presence of a silent and understanding listener.

With Belle for many hours I was as chary of talking as if I were doling out drops of water to someone on the verge of dying from thirst. She entered treatment at the age of twenty-six. Her husband was an irascible man, considerably older than herself, whose first wife had ended her life in a mental hospital. Belle was the stepmother of two malad-justed children.

During her first year of psychotherapy, she "talked herself out," as she later expressed it. I just listened. Once in a while she let me know that she thought my silence was "very funny," but these comments were purely provocative. She went right on talking and made no real effort to establish contact with me. My rare questions seemed to hurt her.

"I talked to you in your office an hour a week and in my mind the rest of the week," she said when she was close to recovery. "You didn't try to give me any information or ideas about myself. For the first time in my life, I was with someone who was willing to just let me talk."

At first Belle was so disoriented that it was hard to figure out what she was saying about herself. She spoke disjointedly and frequently drowned her thoughts in the torrent of words. But the more she talked, the more logical and sensible she sounded. The improvement in her condition at the end of a year was phenomenal; before the end of the second year, she had left treatment, a remarkably well woman.

Belle had first presented herself as a person who had trouble getting along with people. She had mentioned her embroilments as a child with her brothers and sisters. Eventually, though, I got to understand that this was not her fundamental problem. It was, rather, one of getting a word in edgewise and being listened to. Although totally unaware of this herself, she gave me the first clue to the situation when she said: "I was the youngest child in a large family." What she needed most was the opportunity to learn how to assert herself. She was one of those persons who can acquire insight simply by verbalizing her thoughts and feelings in the presence of an ever-willing listener whom she was confident would understand her.

In one fairly simple case, recovery meant outgrowing a tendency to swallow anger. I worked with Martin for many hours helping him acquire the capacity to release his angry feelings in words, but I was not at hand to witness his instantaneous cure.

I encountered him for the first time while making hospital rounds. A burly young man with a pasty complexion and weak smile listened quietly while I talked to some of his ward mates. Then he stopped me at his bedside to talk about his gastric ulcers, the reason for his third hospital confinement in less than two years. He had heard that ulcers could be cleared up through psychiatric treatment. Would I be willing to treat him, he asked, and would this mean that he could do without an operation?

Sometimes this was possible, I told him. We could try in his case if the hospital permitted it and if he was willing to co-operate. The necessary arrangements were made, and the young shipping clerk entered psychotherapy. Three times a week we worked to clear away the obstacles to the verbal release of the angry feelings with which he attacked his stomach.

A year and a half later, he lost his job after a violent argument with his boss. The day he reported the incident to me, Martin was horribly ashamed of his explosive behavior, aghast at what he had told the other man, and still stunned by the aftermath.

"After the boss fired me for his own mistake, I told him off in every four-letter word I knew," Martin said. "Then I felt awful about it and wanted to eat myself to death. I went to a delicatessen and ate three suicidal sandwiches— hot pastrami double-deckers with sour pickles and beer. One of these sandwiches used to be my ruination, but you must have given me an iron stomach. I had no indigestion at all. But now it's my head that is killing me. It feels horrible."

This dramatic recovery from his ulcers was apparently permanent. In the many years that have passed since that episode, there has been no recurrence of his stomach difficulties. But before Martin could leave treatment, we had to contend with the depression which took their place. In the next six months, he conquered that too.

In the course of his treatment, he developed new sensibilities and learned healthful new ways of giving vent to his emotions. Above all, Martin resolved the underlying conflict which had led to his ulcers and then to his psychological disturbance. He achieved sufficient understanding of himself to satisfy both of us, as well as his family and friends, that he had become a well-adjusted person. He was satisfied with his work, and, in general, his life abetted his treatment. He had a pleasant home and social life. He married within a year after his case was closed.

For one reason or another, recovery is a more difficult process for some patients. Consistently unfavorable life experiences can defeat my most strenuous and time-consuming efforts to achieve basic personality change. The story of Edith, the depressed widow of my first group, illustrates this point. I have already related her early history and described the vicissitudes of her treatment. After being discharged from the mental institution where I first saw her and after developing a good relationship with me, she became well enough to support herself thereafter and retain command of her life.

Whenever reality was not too unbearable for this very sensitive and mixed-up woman, she seemed to be sufficiently improved to do without the bolstering effects of treatment. Then someone else close to her died. Tragedy stalked her so persistently that she was unable to stabilize her improvement and become a really sturdy, integrated, and flexible personality. Eventually, I discharged her from treatment, after she had formed a good attachment to her niece. But hers was a case in which I was forced to lower my sights from substantial emotional growth to so-called social recovery.

This is an important way station on the road to complete recovery. The person who reaches that point gets along fairly well thenceforth under normal circumstances, but may break down again should his life become unduly stressful. Though not well in the true sense of the word, he is able to accommodate himself to the immediate demands of his situation. If he was too incapacitated to work at all earlier in treatment, he now holds a job without difficulty. If he had managed to work with some degree of discomfort, he now finds work easy and may even enjoy it. If he was severely ill and relatives have been paying for his treatment by a private practitioner, he is now generally able to earn enough money to pay for it himself.

Persons suffering from severe psychoneuroses usually achieve social recovery in two years; those with psychotic conditions require from two to five.

Complete recovery spells substantial emotional growth and immunity against the recurrence of the illness. It may take up to five years in a severe neurotic condition, and possibly twice as long for the person suffering from a psychotic condition, stemming from emotional damage during the first few months of life. A simple psychoneurotic illness usually responds to two years of treatment, but those who suffer from one rarely enter treatment today.

My ultimate objective in a case is to produce curative inner change. In other words, to clear up the emotional tendencies that are leading the patient toward failure, to immunize him against further illness, and to increase his capacity for happiness and self-fulfillment.

The tendencies which have interfered with efficient and pleasurable functioning in life always show up in individual and group psychotherapy. They are resolved as resistances to emotionally significant verbal communication. Their resolution does not necessarily mean that he has been relieved of all his problems or that he will not encounter new ones later on. Analytic psychotherapy is not a cure-all, nor does it guarantee a charmed future.

A wholly favorable outcome does signify that he has

the ability to feel, think, and behave appropriately in all normal situations and to meet the impact of abnormally traumatic ones with considerable resiliency. He has sufficient understanding of himself and others to serve thereafter as his own analyst, and to deal independently with conflicts of ordinary magnitude. In other words, the case closes with the emergence of an emotionally mature personality. That is my own concept of cure, recovery, or whatever other term one may wish to apply to such an outcome.

The mature person is emotionally versatile. That is, he has the capacity to act spontaneously in socially desirable ways and to respond appropriately to the behavior and emotions of other people. The development of feelings which promote good functioning is therefore an important aspect of the recovery process.

Feelings facilitate behavior. The fact that we feel like doing something helps us to do it. It is, for example, much easier to work when we feel like working than when we feel like loafing, as all of us do at times. We often struggle against the feeling of laziness; but if we are sensible we also give into it when we need rest and relaxation. If we insist on working when our feelings cry out to us to stop, our work suffers the consequences. That is a serious handicap which I have observed in many of my patients. They fight habitually against the feeling of laziness, instead of realistically indulging it on occasion. As a result it dominates their functioning and makes it much harder for them to accomplish their objectives. Accordingly, they have to learn to heed their feelings.

The emotionally immature person tends to be bogged down in the basic and essentially gross feelings with which he started out in life. As his early transference reactions indicate, the extreme feelings of his childhood still trouble him. If the parent he talks about is not "very good," he must be "very bad." At the beginning of treatment, alone with me or in a group, he plays the same tune over and over again, like an old-fashioned music box.

One woman complained at first of an absence of feelings. She was incapable of feeling love for others or their love for her, she said. A scholarly and introspective person, she became aware of many new feelings during the next few years. She described each of them to me as it "came in."

One after another, she identified feelings of being disturbed, of being suspicious of me, of emptiness, uncertainty, pain, and anxiety. Next in the sequence were feelings of confidence and of respect for my mental abilty. Later she said: "I'm just beginning to feel that you won't kick me out of here or harm me." Then she acquired the feeling that she could trust me not to retaliate if she dared to get angry; after verbalizing her anger, she felt hatred for me. After a while she said that she felt attracted to me. Her next new feeling was that she would like to spend more time with me. Feelings that she loved me, that I would welcome her love, and that I accepted it were the next to awaken. Not long after that, she announced: "Now I'm beginning to feel loved myself—very warm inside."

As the hierarchy of feelings which characterize emotional evolution develop, the personality becomes more richly textured. This enables the patient to be more discerning and sensitive. His original gross feelings are refined and distilled into progressively more discriminatory feelings. Eventually he commands an enormous repertory of feelings. These appear appropriately to produce the feeling-tones pertinent to each occasion, much as the instruments of the orchestra combine to produce the precise tone combinations which the score and the conductor's baton call for. I like to think of the emotionally mature personality as the well-orchestrated personality.

Recovery would be much simpler if patients could shed their troublesome feelings in response to suggestion, persuasion, coaxing, or a little cracker-barrel philosophy. Personal influence often does dispel these feelings temporarily; but this is so-called transference cure, which may not last any longer than our relationship. For permanent improvement, the undesirable feelings have to be understood and worked through, until, in the course of their modification and refinement, they are outgrown and displaced by more appropriate feelings.

The impact of other patients' feelings often helps a group member modify his own. One seriously disturbed man, himself the product of a broken home, was on bad terms with his wife when his group treatment began. He reported a dream about a bitter quarrel between his parents, who had been divorced in his childhood. "In the dream, I was about the age I am now," he told the group. "Mother was telling father that he had never done anything for her. I defended him; I said that he had done the best he could. I felt very sad; I could feel myself weeping because they were divorced. I awoke with a groan. My wife has often told me the same thing that my mother told my father in that dream."

The affection and concern of other group members helped to distill in him new feelings of family acceptance. These helped him deal more successfully with his chronic family and business anxieties. Changes in feeling lead to changes in functioning; the reverse is also true. Later he told the group that he had greatly resented his parents' divorce and feared that he himself might be divorced.

"But new feelings should displace old feelings," he said. "It isn't important that I once felt destitute without my mother. Now I am independent of her and happy with my wife. We get along much better now."

Many persons cling to the feelings with which they are most familiar; however troublesome, breaking the attachment seems even more painful. Coming out of a depression, one woman told her group, was "horribly upsetting"; she felt as if she were losing her best friend. Those who have experienced unbearable sensations in response to the hostile feelings of other people also struggle against giving up their unhealthy defenses against feeling anything, especially hostility. After they have unconsciously prevented themselves from acting destructively by numbing their feelings or counteracting them with other feelings, it is difficult to recondition themselves to feel and express their own hatred.

Few patients commit themselves fully to the frustrating process of curative inner change when they enter psychotherapy. They generally feel a strong need for some change in their *status quo*, but approach it as some superficial improvement. "Improvement" may mean no more than satisfying some psychological need or alleviating a painful symptom.

Patients whose lives are drab and lonely characteristically take the attitude that the group experience is designed to satisfy their intense hunger for excitement. One man called it his only pleasure. Financially and emotionally, his work was unrewarding; it kept him immersed in petty and monotonous tasks. The excitement of the group activity helped him function better. "It keeps me going," he said. Other than dealing with his fatiguability, he was uncertain at the beginning what else he wanted to accomplish.

On the other hand, those whose activities keep them humming want to utilize the group sessions chiefly to relieve their tensions. One woman arrived each week with some current problem to get "off her chest" as hastily as possible. After unburdening herself, she would benefit from the ensuing discussion of her problem. For some time, however, she fought against having feelings for the other members of the group or becoming aware of their feelings for her.

Most new patients are primarily concerned with being relieved of their painful symptoms, such as feelings of fright, headaches, insomnia, bodily tension, or compulsive rituals. They start off with the plea: Make me feel better right away. Like the animal that gnaws off a leg to escape from a trap, they want to proceed in whatever way will bring them the most speedy relief.

On that score, there can be a real conflict of interest between us. I do not try to relieve symptoms directly; their alleviation is of little significance for the final outcome. I focus consistently on the emotional conflict. If this is dealt with therapeutically, the symptoms and the other by-products of the conflict disappear sooner or later. Some do so after the basic disturbance has been resolved, the way blighted leaves fall off a tree that has already recovered from some disease process. More frequently, symptoms are greatly alleviated or disappear early in treatment, especially in the group setting.

Too much relief too early in treatment is generally undesirable. If symptoms or superficial disabilities disappear too rapidly, the patient's interest in getting to the roots of his problems tends to evaporate. I structure the treatment sessions so that he will develop real concern about whatever is necessary to achieve permanent inner change. I try to keep him in a state of mild discomfort—neither so much that he will be tempted to give up the struggle, nor so little that he will have no incentive to struggle for more comfort.

He may chafe at the discomfort. One man complained: "You don't care how I feel. To you the important thing is the end result. That's important to me, too, but I don't want to wait that long to feel good. I want to feel good now, while you're treating me. Today."

This attitude is harder to contend with in a group than in individual treatment. Typically, a patient responds more quickly to the group setting. His co-patients give him a new perspective on his problems; these also seem less overwhelming to him as he listens to their reports on their own difficulties. He may not feel as much urgency about tackling his emotional conflict. For that reason, there is a greater danger that the group member will drop out of treatment too early: in other words, before he fully understands the significance of his conflict and what can be done about it.

This happened in the case of Helen, who appeared to improve more rapidly than the other members of my first group. The "terrified virgin" was so impressed with her first feelings of relief and improvement that she insisted on leaving the group after six months. However, she was unable to stabilize the gains she had made. Later she re-entered psychotherapy. She had made a "flight into health"—a type of superficial improvement which represents a powerful obstacle to analytic work.

Feeling better, most patients find out, is not a cue to leave treatment. With some of them, though, I work a long time to create the wish to be cured. This is part of the curative process.

When patients acquire this wish they lose interest in the symptoms which preoccupied them when they entered treatment. Some stop talking about the symptoms altogether. Early in her group experience, one woman frequently discussed the phobia she had about riding in the

subway and the inconvenience it caused her. After she became absorbed in understanding her emotional difficulties
with her husband, she rarely referred to her phobia. Half a
year later, she casually mentioned that she had been using
the subway regularly for months. "Didn't I tell you?" she
asked when one of the other patients expressed surprise.

Some patients get to feel a great deal worse in the course
of their treatment before they begin to feel better. One
group member introduced himself to his co-patients as
a "perfectly contented guy outside my office." Aside from
an irritating slowdown in his work, nothing troubled him.
He told them during the first session that he felt fine. Later
on, he became aware that he had a serious family problem
and evidenced growing concern over it. The more pressure
he experienced to understand himself, the more miserable
he felt. At a time when I considered him very much better
and he was repeatedly demonstrating his improved functioning, he told the group that he had never felt worse.

I treated a severely depressed woman who weighed 205
pounds when I first saw her. She said she wanted to lose
75 pounds. A year and a half later she tipped the scales at
130 pounds and maintained her weight at that level. However, her improved health and appearance gave her little
satisfaction. For nearly a year, her feelings lagged behind
the physical change. "I still feel like 205 pounds," she often
lamented.

Some people cling desperately to feelings they have outgrown. They seem stunned when I tell them that they are
close to recovery. Its approach brings frightening prospects
of exploring the unknown—the new life that is about to
begin.

The most direct and trustworthy evidence I have on a
patient's recovery is his behavior in his sessions. During

the final phase of his treatment, I subject him to a variety of pressures to determine the extent and the permanence of the progress he has demonstrated. I investigate his ability to cope with the kinds of situations which caused him the most difficulty when he entered psychotherapy. He reports what members of his family or close associates are saying about his behavior; their comments are discussed. By the time he conducts himself in a wholly co-operative and realistic way in his therapy sessions, he usually is capable of behaving similarly well in the various situations of his life.

In individual treatment, of course, I have only to evaluate how well a patient functions with me. The group setting affords me additional and often more impressive direct evidence—how well he functions with his co-patients. Despite the handicap of having to analyze more persons and situations, I find it easier to assess progress in a group.

It is also probable that a group assessment is less subject to error. In individual treatment my own feelings about a patient may figure largely in a decision that he is ready for discharge. The quality of our relationship may create in me a strong emotional conviction that he has recovered even though his behavior does not indicate much improvement.

In the group, behavior becomes a more important touchstone than my personal impressions. Interaction with other group members subjects a patient to a more severe test and also delineates his behavior much more clearly. Besides, the group gives him the benefit of a "trial by jury." The impressions of his co-patients usually add validity to the judgment rendered. They have witnessed his behavior for many hours. Their eyes and ears are quick to detect changes. Evidence of backsliding is not apt to escape them; on the other hand, they usually react reassuringly when they note some sign of improvement. The group member under examination is less inclined to quibble about any doubts I may express on his fitness to terminate treatment when other members of the group share my opinion. Sometimes they are harder to satisfy!

My concept of co-operative and realistic behavior has various facets. It means, for example, that a patient functions democratically with his co-patients; he recognizes the right of each member of the group to talk and to listen. He gives some evidence that he recognizes the value of belonging to the group. His behavior demonstrates that he has derived some benefit from talking about his own emotional problems as well as from listening while other members of the group talked about theirs; he has also profited from the discussions which have followed their individual disclosures. He recognizes the universality of emotional problems. He is aware of the different perspectives and attitudes which exist among the group members, and he is able to understand and respect these differences. The only point on which he may agree with them is that each of them has the right to disagree.

Paula was a member of a group which was conducted to achieve the objectives I have just mentioned. The attitudes and behavior of the five other members of the group also changed substantially in the course of treatment, but each of them achieved results as different as the difficulties which brought them into treatment. I shall not attempt to describe their concurrent development. What follows is simply the story of Paula.

When she entered individual treatment at the age of twenty-seven, she was tearful, sullen, and gloomy. Although she was tall and slim, with good features and jet-black hair, the harsh look of defeat on her face and her tawdry clothes made her appear coarse rather than attractive.

An only child, she described herself as alone in the world. A close and stormy relationship with her mother had ended with the latter's death two years earlier. Her father, though still living, was in a comatose condition following an operation for a brain tumor; he died a few months later. Paula hated her employer and the secretarial work she was doing, but she had no confidence that she could get the kind of job she wanted. She got along poorly with her office associates and bemoaned her lack of friends.

Paula's mixed feelings for her parents tortured her. It took her a long time to understand and accept the fact that she felt hatred along with love and grief. Her fundamental problem was an insatiable craving for attention. In the transference relationship, she behaved as she had with her mother, a domineering woman who had difficulty raising her. During Paula's sessions on the couch, I envisioned her as a most uncomfortable infant, keeping very quiet until her hunger became excruciating and then wailing incessantly for nourishment. Apparently responding to her mother's feelings of guilt and irritation while feeding her, the infant again became excessively quiet.

Until her mother's death, overcloseness to her and separation from her had been equally intolerable to Paula. She had not learned how to maintain a comfortable psychological distance between herself and other people. Her neurotic pattern was one of provoking attack by her demanding attitude and then running away from it.

I responded to this pattern by giving her graduated doses of silence, to build up her tolerance to frustration. Since she did not get the attack to which she had been conditioned, however much she persevered in her demands, she came to recognize me as an ally who could help her become more reasonable. Her treatment was, in essence, a process of growing up from a very impulsive baby, intolerant of frustration and totally unaware of what went on around her, to a disciplined person with some understanding of her own needs and those of other people.

At first she was excessively preoccupied with herself, withdrawn and moody. She wanted me to dispel her troublesome feelings quickly by some hocus-pocus and help her carry through an ambitious program for bettering her life. The idea that a great deal of effort on her part would be involved in a favorable outcome sank in slowly. She was a most recalcitrant patient, defying instructions and showing little respect for my opinions. She said she would do as she pleased between her sessions.

Although her unco-operative attitude made for slow progress, which she frequently complained about, Paula experienced considerable relief after two years. She talked freely about her feelings. She had become a more outgoing and self-assertive person. She looked younger and more attractive than on her first visit.

Her forward movement in individual psychotherapy was reflected primarily in the energetic and determined way she went about improving her economic status and finding the kind of work she wanted to do. Paula eventually found it in a new firm distributing vitamin products. She decided to settle down there and grow with the firm. She started out by making an outstanding record as a saleswoman. After demonstrating her business acumen in other posts, she was placed in charge of sales promotion.

In her personal life, she was less successful. Three love affairs, one after another, with married men caused her a great deal of anguished soul-searching. She would part with a lover "forever" and then report, a few weeks later, that the affair was "on again." Immersed as she was in the excitement of a reunion or the throes of a departure, she cut herself off from normal social contacts with unmarried men and women of her own age. She pleaded for further help in learning to discipline herself. She said she wanted to get married.

I recommended that Paula complete her treatment in a group primarily because I believed that it would help her understand the social implications of this repetitive behavior. There were other reasons why I favored the transfer. Paula had been in individual treatment for about five years. It began with weekly sessions; when she became financially secure and more involved in treatment these were increased to two or three a week. While she complained about the time it was taking, she unconsciously wanted to make it a more or less permanent relationship. I considered it advisable to place her in a situation where she would have to take more responsibility for her progress. It was likely, too, that contact with other patients would give her the perspective on her own personality and the understanding of other people which she lacked.

She agreed to "polish off" her treatment in the new group I recommended that she join; but the proposal came as a great shock to her, Paula said. "I would have stayed on here forever just to get love."

I told her that she might get it in the group. "Maybe so," she said. "But I wouldn't need any group if I had found a man who loved me and married him."

"Love and marriage make you a part of the social group," I answered. "What I am recommending to you is not a substitute but training for it."

Paula's group mates—two women and three men—had all had some individual psychotherapy, with other analysts or myself. Emily, thirty-three and recently divorced, was a small blond woman who operated a kindergarten. She had difficulty talking about feelings which troubled her. Harriet, a laboratory technician, had trouble talking about any of her feelings. She was forty, unmarried, and absorbed in herself. Raymond and Peter were bachelors in their late thirties. Raymond, an engineer, hoped that the group experience would help him become less shy and awkward with women. Peter, a lawyer and cynic, generally concealed his feelings. Arthur, a few years older and the least controlled of the three men, was an insurance executive, married, and the father of three children. He worried about slowing down in his work and friction with business associates.

Though emotionally constricted to varying degrees, the five of them were well-disciplined persons. They hoped through group process to learn to speak about themselves more spontaneously and to behave more naturally. As they began to interact with Paula, her emotionality made all of them seem pallid.

She spent her first month in the group campaigning for special status. What was she doing there anyway? She knew too much, and the others knew too little, about feelings so she would not permit them to try to analyze her. Her remaining trouble was very simple: always a patient, never a bride. She had really outgrown the patient stage during her individual analysis. It had been thorough and gone deep; all that remained was "top stuff." She should therefore be excused from telling the story of her life. She wanted to concentrate on learning how to discipline herself and to act like a mature person.

"Why don't you then?" Emily asked her. "You talk so much we can't get a word in edgewise. And your hollering gives me a headache."

"I'm very proud to be able to say whatever I feel," Paula

asserted, "and Dr. Spotnitz is proud of me for it. That was one of the things I accomplished in my analysis."

"You mean screaming at everyone who talks to you?" Arthur was contemptuous.

"Do you really think that the leader of this group will permit you to make your own ground rules?" Peter asked. "If you do, you're a dope, and sicker than you think."

"Stop this nonsense or I'll quit." Paula was now in high dudgeon. "How dare you call me sick and dopey?"

"If you're not, why can't you take our hostility?" Raymond questioned her more gently.

The frustrations of the group situation had revived her neurotic pattern with surprising rapidity. Her battle for top billing waxed and waned through many sessions. She cut off other speakers with naïve explanations of their problems, or to contradict what they were saying. She didn't understand why she grated on their nerves and protested that she was only trying to be helpful. Stung by their unfavorable reactions, she would sulk and grieve. "Talk to someone else," she would say when they tried to draw her out of a long silence. By shifting from one extreme to the other, Paula provoked the attack through which she learned to discipline herself. Group process eventually moved her into a more moderate position.

Nevertheless, learning to function appropriately was a painful experience for many reasons. One was her violent objection to being criticized or attacked. She could dish out hostility to others, but she herself hated the taste of it. She wanted a steady diet of expressions of love, and she thought it would be therapeutic. Initially, she took the attitude that the group members were working to *overcome* all negative feelings for each other, rather than to "tame" them in words and get to understand them. Some happy day in the future, she believed, they would convince me that they felt only love and then I would discharge them as "cured." Instead of quietly accepting the angry feelings she provoked, she would act in such a way as to invite further attack. When it came, she would become enraged and threaten to leave.

"This group lacerates me," Paula complained. "My ego isn't strong enough to take this sadism. Besides, drawing blood isn't constructive. If I can't say anything here without starting a revolution, I'm quitting."

But she did not blackmail the group into permitting her to have her own way. The other patients took her threats calmly. On one occasion when she said she was leaving, Arthur told her: "Don't leave by the door. The window's much nearer."

After a session in which she announced she was "through," she would leave my office as if forever. The following week, her arrival would take on the appearance of a sudden renewal. Actually she never missed a session. In her more subdued moods she would apologize for the scenes she made.

"We are here just as symbols to each other," she said during the early period of treatment. Paula liked to juggle with analytic concepts. "Act out what you feel toward your parents," she advised her co-patients, "and then your unconscious will meet your conscious." The melodramatic flavor of some of her pronouncements and the earnestness with which she delivered them won her the title of "analytic career woman." In painful moments, she would ask: "Can't you realize that I'm living and dying and giving up my parents?"

It took her many hours to get to know what the other patients were like. When her fantasies of shadow-boxing with good and bad parents faded, she began to relate to them more realistically. She first recognized that her provocative behavior generated distinctively different responses in each of her associates. Then she recognized the changes in their attitudes to her. As she became more perceptive, she showed more interest in what they had to say. She found many of their comments about herself helpful, and they expressed appreciation for her attempts to co-operate with them. The more satisfaction she got from listening to them, the easier it became for her to share time and attention.

Unconsciously, Paula claimed the distinction of being the "sex girl" of the group. She was forthright in discussing her intimate experiences with men. Each of the other women usually "paired off" with the same man in group situations, but Paula distributed her tender feelings more indiscriminately. Whichever man paid her the most attention in a session seemed to be the most attractive to her. She worked zealously to command attention and to steer the group away from topics which bored her. She became impatient when two of the men explored their feelings about homosexuality. "What's the value of such a discussion?" she asked them.

During one of her disclosures about her love life, she mentioned that she enjoyed "having sex" three times a night. The response of the three male patients in the group must have been highly gratifying to Paula. The following week, she said that she found the group sessions very therapeutic.

During her first year in the group, Paula's disclosures of her current difficulties focused almost exclusively on her relations with Walter. She did not at first regard her affair with him as a problem. He was the executive of a relief agency whom she had recently met while arranging for a contribution of vitamin products to his agency. She was in love with him, she reported, and she thought he loved her. He had warned her that he was a bachelor "by principle," when the affair started.

"Don't you want to get married?" Emily asked.

"I've told you I do," Paula answered. "I intend to marry Walter."

"Getting entangled with a man who tells you he's a bachelor by choice is a peculiar way to get a husband," Arthur snorted. "Here we go again."

"This is different." Paula sounded confident. "He'll change his mind. I'm terrific in bed and he says so. I feel sure he'll never give me up."

"When are you going to stop feeling and think for a change?" Peter sounded weary.

"When you stop thinking and feel for a change," she flared up.

Again Peter spoke up in his controlled way, checking his anger. "What a bitch!"

"Thank you." Paula's voice was cool. "Everybody wants orgasms. That's the basic thing. If I stay this way, I'll get married."

A month later Paula changed her mind. Walter and she had quarreled and parted. Tearfully, she pleaded for compassion. "In my own neurotic way I love him," she said. "But I'm mature enough to break off destructive relationships." For the first time, she said, she really understood what I meant about sublimating her sex drive and learning to discipline herself. A few weeks later, she was seeing "that man" again. Maybe she was a sex addict, but she couldn't give him up. And so it went for nearly a year.

It was Paula's fantasy, when the affair was "on," that marriage would be the solution to all her problems. In appreciation of her wonderful orgiastic activities, Walter would become an attentive husband and give her everything she wanted—above all, the privilege of being a big baby twenty-four hours a day.

When she began to talk about her wild sex life, I suggested that she might curb it. I told her that it might be delaying her improvement. It has been my observation that sexual promiscuity is apt to interfere with psychotherapy. Paula reacted defiantly whenever I made this suggestion. It was incredible; I didn't mean it; I must be crazy; no man would ever go out with her again. These were some of her responses which I studied during that period.

Her co-patients were genuinely concerned with helping her manage her life. They tried to persuade her to behave more sensibly; she was advised and lectured, for example, on changing her tactics with men. My concern, meanwhile, was wholly with the unconscious conflict. Were she to marry before this was resolved, it seemed pretty certain to me that she would be back in treatment some day complaining of marital problems. I concentrated on clearing away the various obstacles which prevented her from functioning healthfully in the treatment setting.

It was her interaction with the other group members, especially the men, that eventually convinced Paula that being a thrilling, loving baby was not a successful formula for adult living. She experienced a variety of emotions for each of the three men—love, jealousy, humiliation, anger, shame, hatred, and rage. Later she got to recognize the many different feelings she aroused in them. She discovered, for example, that though they found her very attractive, they hated her incessant clamoring for attention. It also became clear to her that her sincerity, genuineness, and warm responsiveness to their needs often attracted them more than her physical appeal. With the two women, too, Paula un-

derwent many emotional episodes. She frequently wrestled
with jealousy. "A terrible chill is going through me," she
once exclaimed when Emily captured the spotlight from
her.

Getting to understand the men's attitudes helped her to
modify her own. What she primarily wanted from men,
Paula told the group, was intimacy, tenderness, and companionship. She had tried to "sell" sexual excitement because
she felt that was all men wanted from her. She was too
worthwhile a person to continue this kind of trading. When
she finally ended her affair with Walter she told the group:
"I want to be something more than a good lay."

From time to time, Paula's unconscious operated like a
genius to move her back in the direction from which she had
started. Suddenly the mature woman operating on a high
level of efficiency—the way she functioned in her office
—would act like a squalling baby again. Recovery is never
a straightforward move in one direction. But none of the
spurts backward lasted very long; and finally the balance
stopped shifting backward and forward. She became much
less demanding, and outgrew her most infantile attitudes.

Paula began to "feel cured" as the end of her second year
in the group drew near. "I'm just beginning to live," she
asserted. But her claims to complete recovery were not seriously entertained until she had demonstrated efficient functioning in a variety of group encounters. Her co-patients
expressed many different opinions about her behavior during
the final stage of her treatment. Some of them supported,
others rejected her claims. Peter remarked: "Well, you're
certainly not trying to run this group any more." Emily,
commenting on one of Paula's statements, said: "What you
just said makes me feel that you still have something to
learn about other people." Paula was told that she was taking

criticism in better spirit. And so it went until all of them agreed with me and with each other that she had achieved the goals of her treatment.

But this did not take place until nearly a year after she had begun to "feel cured." During that last year, I studied her behavior in the sessions closely and asked myself various questions about her.

Did she express her emotions spontaneously and clearly? Did her mind and body function in unison? Did she appear thoroughly at ease in all group situations? Had she become objective enough to see herself as the other members of her group saw her? Did she respect her own worth and theirs? Did she have a realistic view of herself as a member of society? When I can answer questions such as these in the affirmative, I am usually satisfied that the group experience has fully served its purpose.

In Paula's case, I could have given yes answers to the first two questions when she entered the group. She was highly proficient in verbalizing her thoughts and feelings. Even when they pained her deeply, she poured them out without any hesitation.

I recalled the time, several months earlier, when she had made the last of her many threats to leave the group. Failing to recognize how upset Raymond was, and how earnestly he was discussing one of his major problems, she said to him: "Feel your feelings, and don't talk about such superficial things." Criticized harshly for it, Paula started to cry and said she was quitting.

"Another threat?" Emily groaned. "Tell us what really bothers you."

"I'm unhappy because it's so hard for me to love people who are hateful to me," Paula declared. "I was terribly depressed today, and now you've made it worse. That's why

I want to leave. I know what my panic and depression come from, but it's so much trouble working them through here."

Arthur went on: "I can't give you love all the time, baby. Why can't you admit that it's normal to have mixed feelings for people?"

She knew now that this was one of her problems, Paula said. Sooner or later she resented every man she went with. In one situation or another, they became hostile, and she wanted only love and admiration. "That's why I don't even want men any more," she continued. "I guess I just make a play for them to take them away from other women."

Peter reminded her that she was not the only member of the group who had the right to say so when she was bothered.

"I agree," she answered. "But when you try to explain me, you outsmart and outwit me. That's why I talk about leaving. It makes me sad to think I have been in treatment so long and still feel this way."

Her bodily movements, general behavior, and the statements she made in the sessions were closely attuned to her emotions. Everything she said and did conveyed her feelings spontaneously and naturally. She never dissembled. She created a harmonious wholeness about her presence. She dressed simply but in excellent taste, wearing clothes that showed off her figure to good advantage. Everything about her gave the impression that she wanted to hide nothing.

The other group members took it for granted that Paula had always possessed this well-synthesized appearance, but it was essentially a product of her individual treatment. During the first year in psychotherapy she had been very rigid on the couch. She had kept her legs crossed and held her arms stiffly over her chest. When she began to make some real headway in understanding herself, this rigidity disappeared; and she gave many signs of being well adjusted when she entered the group.

She was especially sensitive to the localized inhibitions of her co-patients. They were irritated at times to be told that they kept their hands in their pockets, frowned, slouched, or bit their nails, but they found her observations helpful. She stimulated them to investigate habits of which they had not been aware.

Did she always appear at ease in interaction with the other patients? Not until she fully outgrew her hypersensitivity to criticism. She functioned inefficiently under any form of verbal attack. It was frequently pointed out to her that she provoked the tongue lashings she received, and that these constituted socially acceptable reactions.

During the last half year of treatment, Paula handled herself well, whether she was talking or listening. She made few demands for attention. Since criticism no longer made her feel isolated and inferior, she took it good-naturedly instead of trying to demonstrate her "smartness."

I like a patient leaving group treatment to be objective enough to see himself as his co-patients see him. I hope that he has learned how to compare and evaluate their perceptions of him with his own perceptions of himself, and has benefited from making the comparison.

Paula repeatedly demonstrated that she had no perspective on how her actions appeared to others. She frequently maintained, for example, that she was qualified to leave the group, but was never able to say why. Confronted with objective evaluations of her need for further treatment, she would cling to the idea that she *felt* cured. She experienced her feelings as infallible messages from heaven.

When she was asked if she had behaved rationally in a

specific group situation, she would reply that she always knew when she did "nutty" things in the group and why. She did them, she asserted, to get practice in disciplining herself. Besides, she did not behave that way any more outside the group. She would then be reminded of some "horrible mess" she had talked about.

The other patients helped her recognize the unreliability of her own impressions of her actions. She showed increasing appreciation of their opinions of her behavior, and often solicited them. During the last few months of her treatment, a mild reminder that her feelings often misled her would cause her to stop short and reconsider some action she contemplated. By that time she realized that, although her feelings were always a clue to something going on, it might be going on only in her own mind. Hence, she ceased to regard her feelings as trustworthy guides to behavior, and became more reasonable.

The patient who is ready to leave the group usually has respect for his own worth and appreciation of that of his co-members. He understands and respects their attitudes even when he does not agree with them.

Paula was oblivious to other people when she entered individual psychotherapy. She was almost as self-centered during her first six months in the group. Rather quickly, she attached her own feelings to her co-patients. Initially, she was convinced that all of them had the same problems, interests, and objectives. Concerned as she was about becoming a more controlled person, she found it hard to accept the idea that they were relatively well-disciplined persons who were there to explore their feelings and develop new ones. Some of them were self-sacrificing personalities, but she repeatedly stated: "We are all selfish." She also operated on the assumption—indeed, the feeling—that she could persuade them to accept her point of view if they knew how much she wanted them to agree with her.

After she got to know them better and developed an interest in them, for one reason or another things which were important to her co-patients also became important to Paula. Their feelings helped to release her from the grip of her anticipatory attitudes and feelings. Thereafter, she had fewer difficulties in getting along with people generally. Psychologically, her group mates fed her in many ways.

The discovery that they benefited from her emotionality helped to build up her confidence in herself. Her efforts to help Raymond improve his posture and diction led to many discussions about her advice on such matters. His frequent comments on her good grooming and other praise given her made her feel more worth-while. During her last few months in the group, she functioned as an accepted equal.

Paula became more realistic and more discriminating about herself and her co-patients. The fact that they possessed knowledge and experience she did not have about many aspects of life counteracted her notion that she was an exceptionally brilliant woman. Recognition of her own shortcomings and of the admirable qualities of her group mates encouraged her to seek out people. She joined a club for businesswomen and made new friends. She registered for evening courses in art and current events.

As people generally became more significant to her, first in the group and then on her own horizon, her social contacts became more moderate and variegated. Group psychotherapy had gradually eased the impulsive little baby whining "all or nothing" into attitudes befitting an adult.

She told the group that she was becoming more choosy about her male friends. "I fought hard for any jerk when I couldn't stand the idea that I might not get a husband," she said. "Now what I want is a guy who will really love me."

About two and a half years after she left the group, I received a blue-ribboned announcement of the birth of a baby. The family name engraved on the announcement was unfamiliar to me; but on the back, handwritten and signed by Paula, was this cheerful note: "This is our first baby. We are a happy family. My husband is serious and calm and loves people, especially me. A real man, one I've known a long time but never thought was important. Thank you for your help and patience. I'd like the others to know about it. I think of them often and wish I could tell them how much they helped."

Performance in life is, of course, the ultimate test of emotional maturity.

Part · III

THE
PSYCHOTHERAPIST

[9]

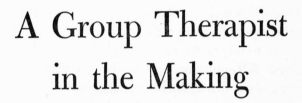

A Group Therapist
in the Making

THE LIFE EXPERIENCES which make people candidates for
analytic group therapy are revealed, sooner or later,
through their personal disclosures and interchanges in the
sessions. The therapist, on the other hand, says little if anything about his own experiences; the phantom figure main-
tains the privacy of his personal identity. Nevertheless, he
does not preserve his anonymity by abstaining from talking
about himself. In countless ways, he proclaims his essence:
his personality, background, and the ideas that guide him.
His life history is implicit in his performance.

The very fact that he treats patients together and looks
to them to help each other through the shared experience
might be interpreted as a confession of inadequacy or as
indicating a need to increase his own effectiveness through
teamwork. He does accept the notion that he can use their
assistance in curing them.

Awareness of one's limitations is an attribute of the mature personality, and a mature personality is a prerequisite for the skillful practice of psychotherapy. The easiest way to achieve emotional maturity is to spend the formative years of life with loving parents who provide gratification and frustration in exquisite balance to foster our emotional growth and ripen our personalities. However, even if our upbringing was ideal in all respects—and few human beings are so fortunate—we cannot consistently employ our personalities in a therapeutic way unless we know and understand ourselves well: our feelings, motives, and the effects of our behavior on other people. That is why, before serving as analysts to others, we undergo individual psychoanalysis ourselves. Self-understanding is the foundation of our training and our first lesson in understanding others.

In the course of our personal analysis, we learn how to counterbalance any adverse effects of our own rearing and later experiences. If these were very damaging, the rectification process may demand more time and effort than if we were brought up with the psychological equivalent of the silver spoon. Hence, the scope of our emotional retraining varies with our individual needs. When it is finished, most of us do not consider that we have signed, sealed, and delivered to ourselves as much knowledge of our own identity as we need. We generally supplement the initial investigation by carrying on a great deal of self-analysis throughout the years of our practice.

Psychoanalytic institutes have tried for many years to define the "ideal" personality for the field. Thus far, they have not had much success either in figuring out the kind of person they should turn out or in predicting the effectiveness of those they do turn out, or turn down for training. Some of their rejected candidates have emerged as out-

standing psychotherapists; others who underwent the training process relatively quickly have become competent and
upright practitioners but without much intuitive perception
of the problems of severely disturbed patients. Knowledge
acquired through suffering and experience in mastering
their own difficulties equip some persons with special awareness of the human organism's capacity for recovery and a
facility for helping it do so.

Individual psychoanalysis, successfully completed, is generally accepted as adequate personality training for those
entering group practice. However, there is growing recognition of the desirability of a group training or treatment
experience. Eventually, this, too, will probably be required.
A higher degree of emotional preparation is needed to conduct analytic psychotherapy comfortably in a group than
in individual practice.

In both settings, the analyst has to understand and deal
appropriately with his so-called countertransference reactions: the feelings and attitudes which he developed as a
child for persons of whom his patients may remind him. If
his own psychoanalysis was successful, he is able to recognize these reactions and prevent them from interfering
with the treatment process. In group practice he has the
additional problem of dealing with powerful emotional currents stimulated by the similar strivings of, say, six or eight
persons—what might be called their common neurosis. He
has to understand any tendencies to swim with or against
these currents as he consciously or unconsciously resists
being swept along by the instinctual forces operating in the
group. In other words, he must recognize, analyze, and
control the various tendencies induced in him by the group
members' impulses, feelings, and behavior. He has to develop the ability to perceive their feelings and his own, and

yet be sufficiently insulated to communicate the responses
they need.

It usually takes ten years from the time he begins his
personal analysis for the practitioner to reach his professional majority in individual treatment. Close to fifteen years
pass before he feels reasonably secure in analytic group
treatment, assuming of course that he conducts it to effect
character change.

Technical knowledge and skills are acquired through
various kinds of professional training. Those of us who
are physicians specializing in psychiatry administer group
psychotherapy as a form of medical healing. We are regarded as legally and morally responsible for diagnosis and
treatment. Our non-medical colleagues, most of whom have
doctoral or other degrees in their own specialty, are likely
to be clinical psychologists or psychiatric social workers.
By and large, the psychotherapists who meet together as
members of the major professional associations in the field
fall into these three categories.

They also work together as "clinic teams" in the mental-
hygiene clinics and other agencies which provide treatment.
The pooling and exchange of knowledge in the course of
these activities give valuable experience to all members of
the team. Working with persons trained in the psychological
and social sciences, for example, gives the psychiatrist a new
perspective on problems in social relationships and in-
creases his skill in handling them. Like many of my medical
colleagues who have served on clinic teams, I learned a great
deal from my associates in treatment—psychiatric social
workers and clinical psychologists. Some of the knowledge
of each team member rubs off on his partners as they co-
operate in treatment.

There is as yet no evidence that the physician, by virtue of his medical background, is a better group psychotherapist than representatives of other professions; or that their training, on the other hand, gives them superior qualifications for this role. Acquisition of all possible theoretical and practical knowledge of each other's field, and especially of group dynamics, is profitable for all of us. But as in individual treatment, factors harder to define seem to be more important than our respective professional training.

I was consulted recently by a young woman who asked me to arbitrate a dispute between herself and her friends about her choice of psychotherapist. Two and a half years earlier, she had entered treatment for a serious emotional disturbance with an internationally known medical psycho-analyst of unquestioned competence. After treating her individually for a few months, she said that he had placed her in one of his groups. She withdrew after a year, in discouragement over her lack of improvement. Shortly afterward, she entered group treatment with a non-medical analyst recommended to her by an acquaintance. She felt that she was making progress in his group and wanted to remain there. Her friends were volubly insistent that she had displayed poor judgment in leaving her first analyst. They were urging her to return to him.

"I don't doubt that he's an excellent man," she told me, "but I just didn't get anywhere with him. I didn't feel that the other patients he put me with gave me anything either. Now things are different. I click with my present analyst, and I have real feelings about the other members of the group. After a few sessions with them, I felt that I was really getting somewhere. But I'm upset by my friends' attitude about my going to a lay analyst. They've made up their minds that I'm being treated by a charlatan; they say I'll waste my time and money if I stick with him. I want your advice as a neutral party."

I asked if she could think of any reason why she should leave her present analyst. She said she could not. He had made no immodest claims about himself, and had not guaranteed results. She was not looking for magic, she added; she knew that successful treatment meant a lot of work for her.

The name of the analyst under discussion was unknown to me, but I found it listed in the membership directories of several national professional organizations, among them the American Group Psychotherapy Association. Colleagues of whom I inquired about the man gave me no information which might have led me to question his competence.

"You seem to have a choice between being a personal failure with a well-known medical analyst and being a personal success with a lay analyst," I told her. "I see no reason why you should return to the first unless you prefer to be a failure again."

Any qualified analytic psychotherapist can give an emotionally disturbed person intellectual understanding of himself, but we have learned that such insight is not in itself curative. What is decisive for his recovery is the emotional relationship which develops when treatment is conducted to meet the particular growth needs of his personality. These cannot be met without the development and exchange of genuine feelings.

Antipathy as well as attraction, even profound dullness may spark feelings; but it is hard for these to develop in a completely indifferent relationship. The kind which can be channeled into emotional growth is not created solely on the basis of intelligence and professional training. Countless tangible and intangible factors, among them hereditary and cultural endowments, personal attitudes, and even voice and mannerisms, influence our functioning. Whatever "school" we may belong to, we tap the reservoir of our own resources somewhat differently to develop a therapeutic personality.

For one whose orientation is analytic, for example, I frequently operate in an unorthodox manner. Though interpretation is the only standard procedure in analytic psychotherapy, I supplement interpretation with other procedures developed in individual psychotherapy. I operate flexibly on the basis of scientific principles, but use my feelings freely in my responses as well as to aid me in my perceptions. This approach grew out of personal characteristics, attitudes, and experiences.

Emotional responsiveness is to some extent inborn, but it is fostered by a lively childhood and by contacts with many people during one's formative years. My own early experiences also help to explain my interest in problems of group living. I grew up in Boston—about a mile away from where Joseph Pratt was conducting his historic tuberculosis class—in an overcrowded area that afforded a vivid foretaste of the smoldering tensions which help to breed emotional disorders. A patient's disclosure about the destructive impact of his childhood surroundings reminds me of the gang wars which terrorized my own neighborhood. A notorious murder took place on the street where I lived. I saw overwrought people bite their hands in rage or assault one another with lead pipes.

In this crime-infested neighborhood, parents like my own struggled to give their children opportunities which they themselves had not enjoyed. As the oldest child of five, I guided the activities and arbitrated the quarrels of my sisters and brothers while my parents worked in their candy store below our home. In my memory they were always working.

My attitudes and feelings during a group session often hark back to the schoolboy who had to act quickly in an emergency while maintaining sufficient detachment to supervise the total activity of four siblings. The role of parental helper in a large family is excellent conditioning for a group therapist. Working and playing in resonance with many feelings, I became keenly aware of personality differences among members of my own family. I recognized my acute sensitivity to feelings when I started to work with severely disturbed patients.

I doubt that anyone chooses to become a physician if he is not interested in helping people recover from illness. But the first time I used a stethoscope, I was more interested in hearing a heart tick than in curing the patient. I was then about five years old, and the family doctor examining my baby sister obligingly helped me satisfy my curiosity.

"He's joining the profession," he explained to my mother. "Yes, he's going to be a doctor," she instantly agreed.

The idea germinated in this way was sedulously nourished during my boyhood, but thoughts of a conventional medical practice never appealed to me. I am still primarily interested in investigating how people tick.

At Boston Public Latin School I had a teacher who inspired me with a love of mathematics that carried over into my work. I enjoyed spending four or five hours at a time working out the solution to an algebra problem. The physical sciences and philosophy also attracted me. But after reading Sinclair Lewis' novel *Arrowsmith* as a freshman at Harvard College, I became more and more enthusiastic about exploring some unknown frontiers in medicine. I decided to be a medical scientist.

When I entered medical school in 1929, I turned to neurology and psychiatry, not because I expected to become a practitioner, but because severe mental illness was then opening up as an important area of exploration. While attending the University of Berlin, I worked as a voluntary research assistant at the Kaiser Wilhelm Institute for Brain Research, where I studied the microscopic structure of the brain. My investigations of nervous and mental functions, which were later carried on at the New York Neurological and Psychiatric Institutes, gradually drew me into the practice of psychotherapy.

I first became interested in it when I learned, in the course of my neurological research, the rationale of talking cures. Speech affects the mind and through the mind's physical structure—the nervous system—the chemistry of the body. I have experimented with pharmacologic treatment, especially insulin shock, and found it nowhere near as effective as psychological medicine, at least in my hands. It would probably take hundreds of years to compound the exquisitely precise chemicals which each patient needs to get well and stay well. But his body has its own chemical laboratory; and the psychotherapist, through his words and attitudes, tries to stimulate it to produce those chemicals. The personality can be employed in an infinite number of ways to create different psychological effects and control the dosages for each patient and situation. To advance the science and art of producing psychological stimuli is the concern of the research-minded practitioner.

When I started my neurological training, Freud's theories and findings on mind-body relationships greatly interested me. I also read psychoanalytic literature avidly at medical school. With a few classmates, I experimented with psychoanalysis as a method of probing the most obscure aspects of mental functioning. While walking or lunching together, we took frequent excursions into hitherto unexplored areas of the mind—each other's and our own.

My amateur ventures in self-analysis, during years spent so far from home, had a value above and beyond that of most intellectual exercise. In the process I accrued some unexpected dividends. Discovery of the origin or significance of an irrational feeling or impulse usually brought me new insight and energy. States of fatigue or tension were often traced back beyond the day's activities to nostalgia and loneliness for my family and close friends from whom I was separated. As I thought about them, feelings of love and of being loved would surge through me. It was not always easy to maintain scientific objectivity under the circumstances, but I did resolve one emotional obscurity after another. And I became convinced that psychoanalysis was an effective tool for investigating the mind and understanding human behavior.

In my psychiatry courses, this tool helped me to penetrate a forbidding diagnostic façade and get to know the human being behind it. The psychiatry taught in those days was oriented to the classification of mental diseases and symptoms; that is, to diagnosis and custodial care rather than to psychological treatment. But the academic description of a patient under study whetted my appetite for exploring his thoughts and feelings. The psychoanalytic approach transformed his hapless behavior and disorganized statements into a fascinating story of why and how he had broken down in health.

Such clues often helped me to put together an accurate

history of an emotional disorder when I began to practice psychiatry, although I had not yet undergone formal training in psychoanalysis. It was heartening to find that I had an instinctive facility for helping a patient resolve the obstacles to healthful functioning. But there was less to learn from someone who responded to standard methods than from treating a severely disturbed person who was regarded as inaccessible to psychotherapy. In fact, I had an intense desire to work with the "hopeless" patient and to help him prove that he wasn't.

That was the spirit in which I embarked on my first intensive case as a pyschiatrist in a mental institution. Chloe, a beautiful young brunette, had been hospitalized following an acute episode of catatonic schizophrenia. Because of my interest in the case, I was invited to take it over by the psychiatrist who had been treating her.

Her family history, as well as her failure to respond to treatment during her first three months in the institution, suggested a bleak outcome to the case. Her mother had committed suicide and her schizophrenic father had died in a mental institution. Chloe herself had started out in life with many emotional problems, for which she had been treated intermittently during her childhood and adolescence at a psychiatric clinic. But she had improved sufficiently to function well for several years in a secretarial job, which she had given up at the time of her marriage to a young engineer. Her breakdown had occurred about five months later. I suspected that it was connected with some incident to which she attached great emotional significance; but her devoted husband could give no information on any difficulties which might have precipitated it.

I started Chloe's treatment under an intense challenge to understand her condition; and I soon developed such a strong drive to cure her that I spent several hours a day five or six days a week on the case. It seemed to me that she would respond if I made a great effort to help her. To show my interest, I laughed whenever she made humorous statements. To my surprise, my earnest attempts to establish some emotional contact with her proved unrewarding. She hurled ash trays in my direction but gave little information.

About two months after I started to treat Chloe, I discussed her case at a staff conference. Among those present was Dr. Karl Menninger, one of the distinguished psychiatrists who frequently visited the institution and informally assisted the psychiatrists there with their cases. After hearing my report, he said to me: "Don't laugh when your patient laughs, or she will feel that you are ridiculing her." Similar suggestions, some made by Dr. Menninger in his hotel room during later visits to New York, contributed a great deal to my understanding of the case, especially the recognition of her laughter and wisecracks as a resistance to verbalizing her great need to destroy herself.

I stopped laughing and simply tried to understand her. My presence frequently enraged her, but, however badly she mistreated me, I stood my ground and maintained sincere interest in the meaning of whatever she said. Eventually, she stopped throwing me off the track and, in a highly dramatic session, began to purge herself of the secret which she had fought against telling me: her guilt about an abortion she had undergone about a month before her breakdown. As I listened to her without displaying any emotion, she cried out: "I didn't want to tell you. I was sure you wouldn't have any use for me if you knew I'd killed my own child!"

A few facts at a time, during the sessions that followed, the story behind her breakdown was assembled. Chloe and her husband had agreed, at her insistence, that she would wait a year before bearing a child. Before the year was half over, she found out that she was pregnant. Enraged, she accused him of tricking her and decided to have an abortion. His reluctance to have her undergo it increased her conviction that he had tricked her. Later she became furious at her husband for having given his permission, as well as at herself for having impulsively gone ahead with the abortion. Her suppressed anger, remorse, and guilt about it precipitated the acute schizophrenic episode. Her husband had not connected it with the abortion because she had concealed her feelings from him; actually she was not aware of them herself. He also made it clear when I spoke with him that he had not impregnated her deliberately.

After the cathartic session in which Chloe began to talk, she was in better contact with reality each time I saw her, though the change was so imperceptible to others at first that I was accused of wishful thinking. However, once her improvement began, it was exceptionally rapid, probably because her illness was recent and acute rather than chronic; moreover, extensive treatment in her earlier years had made her readily amenable to psychotherapy. I attributed her progress to my success in getting her to talk out her hostility, in understanding her behavior and making her aware that I did. The more I understood, the more rational she became.

Six months after I had started to work with her, she was discharged from the hospital as a recovered patient. There has been no recurrence of the illness. Chloe now is the mother of four children and socially prominent in her community.

Parenthetically, Freud's dictum that schizophrenics don't respond to psychoanalytic therapy because they can't be

drawn into an effective treatment relationship has been
contradicted by the reports of a growing number of analysts. But my success with the first case of this nature
strengthened my determination to help make schizophrenia
and other baffling illnesses comprehensible, and to learn how
to meet the special needs of those who suffer from them.
Since then, the study and treatment of these diseases have
gone hand in hand in my practice.

Every young psychotherapist who starts out with an
intense urge to help people get well has to resolve the
crucial issue of how he will do it. Should he make concrete
suggestions to them about improving their behavior, or
should he study it until he is able to understand it and,
eventually, educate them to improve their own functioning? This question suggests two conflicting tendencies in
the field of psychotherapy, which are sometimes referred
to as the "therapeutic attitude" and the "analytic attitude."
Both were reflected to some extent in my treatment of
Chloe.

Before Dr. Menninger intervened in this case, I was
primarily a psychotherapist. I had a strong urge to cure
Chloe through suggestion, persuasion, support, inspiration,
and any similar influences which I could exert on her.
These got me nowhere, and explained the inability of her
first psychiatrist to make headway with her. After I was
helped to recognize the value of understanding her, my approach was different. I stopped trying so hard to help her
and began to analyze her instead. I devoted myself primarily to figuring out why she had broken down and to
giving her the kind of understanding and emotional experience which would restore her to health. Her response
demonstrated the healing possibilities inherent in the psychoanalytic approach.

Usually it takes considerable time for the young therapist to develop confidence in his patient's ability to resolve his difficulties and find his own solutions to conflicts. The therapist may be tempted to shortcut the psychoanalytic process and suggest a good life for a patient, even instruct him how to live it. One analytic group therapist considered issuing a list of rules and directions, until he found out that telling patients how he thought they should conduct themselves was less helpful than conveying his understanding of their behavior and its implications, and permitting them the freedom to utilize this knowledge as they wished. On the other hand, the "analytic attitude" can also be carried to an undesirable extreme. The inexperienced practitioner who is enthusiastic about the value of psychoanalysis may be tempted to impart his understanding of a patient's problems before the latter is able to assimilate such interpretations without feeling more confused or hopeless about himself. The psychotherapist has to learn not only how to analyze but also how to share his understanding therapeutically. The golden mean he seeks to achieve is therapeutic analysis.

In 1940, shortly after treating my first schizophrenic patient, I became a student at the New York Psychoanalytic Institute and soon decided to devote myself entirely to psychoanalytic psychotherapy. My primary motive in studying at the Institute was to learn and test out the classical psychoanalytic procedures taught there and to ascertain their main limitations. These were important for me to know, in order to determine the extent to which the procedures would have to be modified in order to work effectively with patients suffering from severe emotional disorders.

Today, I no longer attempt to operate within the framework of any one method. I base treatment on the major concepts of resistance and transference—Freud's own definition of psychoanalysis—but employ whatever techniques will help to implement these concepts. I try to find out what the individual patient needs and treat him accordingly. I have heard myself described as a follower of Freud, Adler, Sullivan, Rank, Stekel, Theodor Reik, Wilhelm Reich, and others. I was referred to as a follower of Carl Rogers before I had any knowledge of his concepts or procedures.

Effective methods are the product of many schools and many minds. In psychological medicine the practitioner is manifesting a growing tendency to employ whatever procedures will bring the best results, just as the competent practitioner in organic medicine gives the drug that is most beneficial to his patient. If, for example, an upper respiratory infection or pneumonia doesn't respond to one antibiotic, the patient is given another, perhaps several, while it is determined which drug is the best remedy for him. The neurosurgeon, with perhaps a thousand instruments to draw from, chooses those which will be most effective each time he performs an operation.

The armamentarium of the psychotherapist is much less extensive because he works in one of the youngest branches of medical science. The number of methods at his disposal is limited, and to learn any one of them is a time-consuming process. However, with modification of established techniques and the introduction of new procedures, psychotherapy is gradually becoming less rigid.

Had I chosen to restrict myself to the classical method of applying psychoanalytic principles, I suppose that I would not have become a group psychotherapist. Before doing so, I conducted various studies of group processes and results. I also investigated the special demands which group treatment makes on the therapist, in connection with my

training and supervisory activities. The next step was to
enter this new field of practice myself.

From the study of the brain's microscopic structure to
group psychotherapy is truly a leap in the course of one
career; but it was probably inevitable for a research psychiatrist who started to explore severe mental illness thirty
years ago. We have learned since then that the therapy
group is an excellent laboratory in which to study the illness as well as to heal the patient.

In a sense, I practiced group psychotherapy long before
I formed my first group, since some of my individual
patients had been indirectly sharing each other's treatment
experiences, to their mutual benefit. A person who is
getting over a grave emotional disorder is usually eager to
be of some service to others who suffer from one. The
knowledge that he can make a contribution to their progress tends to facilitate his own. He wants to hear about
other patients; when he is close to recovery I may talk
over with him some of my problems in other cases. His
impressions often stimulate me in making my own decisions
about these cases.

There were times at the beginning of my practice when
I scrutinized a new patient and wondered if he was likely
to do physical violence in his sessions. Some patients did.
Schizophrenia is a disease with many frightening aspects.
A little fright makes a case challenging and exciting, but it
is impossible to help a person if one is paralyzed with fear
about how he will respond to the next intervention. Too
much anxiety blocks effective treatment.

Before I recognized that my anxiety was not the patient's
problem but my own, I opened a case with the feeling that
all I had to do to secure good results was to change the
patient. It was rather shocking to discover that I had to

change myself too. Some feelings and attitudes, such as fear of the illness or the patient, hamper his treatment; it also became clear to me that there were others which he needed to experience from me—for example, real feelings of hate and love, and the security of knowing that he was with someone who was genuinely interested in him and comfortable in his presence. When I satisfied these needs, he relaxed and worked more constructively on his problems; and my fears and anxieties evaporated.

But it is impossible to hand out feelings the way a physician gives a drug or other external remedy to someone suffering from an organic illness. I had to develop those feelings in myself. The psychotherapist has to grow into the kind of person who can give his patients the right feelings at the right time.

[10]

Some Group Leaders Talk Shop

A YOUNG PSYCHOLOGIST who does psychotherapy in a child-guidance clinic talked with me one day about the "confusing things we say we do" in working with groups.

"When I read reports of therapists whose training and methods differ from my own, what goes on in their groups is often a mystery to me," said Wanda Green.[1] "The jargon we use and our different philosophical approaches make it hard for us to communicate clearly with each other. This is inevitable, I suppose, because we're such subjective operators. But I have a hunch that if we got together and compared notes, we'd find that we're not as far apart as we sound. At least, we'd be able to understand each other better. By the way, some therapists I know would like to do this. Would you help us exchange experiences on a regular

[1] The names of the psychotherapists quoted in this chapter are pseudonyms.

basis? A sort of research and discussion project, along the lines of your seminars and workshops?"

The upshot of that conversation was the formation, some months later, of the group of six psychotherapists whose opinions and observations are reported in this chapter. One evening a week, for about a year, they came to my office to discuss various group approaches, among them some commonly employed systems of counseling and non-analytic therapy. Their first few "shop talks" were devoted to an overview of the field of group treatment. What follows is based on a reconstruction of the records of those sessions.

"All of us employ psychological procedures that have been in use for many centuries," I said by way of introduction. "The main contribution of the twentieth century is their development into scientific systems of treatment. I understand that you are interested in finding out more about their differences and similarities. Those among you who do non-directive and family counseling, conduct psychodrama, therapeutic social groups, and activity group therapy might serve as unofficial spokesmen for your own systems. How would you like to proceed?"

"Let's start from scratch; that is, assume we know nothing about each other's methods," said Wanda Green. "This ought to help us pin down the unique things we do, and also those we call by different names which really are similar."

"How do you propose doing this?" I asked. "Would formal rules of procedure be helpful for these sessions? Do you want to have theoretical discussions, present cases, or what?"

"Let's agree to operate as democratically as possible without tying ourselves down to directions." The speaker was a calm, friendly-looking man with a somewhat academic manner. Dr. Leslie Gray, a psychologist, was affiliated with a private counseling center which employed the non-directive approach developed by Carl R. Rogers.

"That sounds like a good introduction to your own activity, Les," someone commented. "Why don't you start off?"

"A good suggestion," I told him. "We'd like to hear a firsthand account of the non-directive method."

"It's also called the client-centered method," Dr. Gray said. "Our approach is social rather than medical. People come to us for counseling service and we call them clients. I'll tell you about one of them—a businessman I shall call Roger. He has been in one of my groups for about a year."

Dr. Gray provided this preliminary information: His client was a thin, saturnine man in his mid-thirties, the executive vice-president of an oil company. During his initial consultation, he stated that his problems were not serious but that a business associate had suggested that he might benefit from talking them over with someone at the counseling center. Roger explained that he was experiencing increasing difficulty in co-ordinating his business and domestic life. He was married and lived with his wife and ten-year-old son in a suburban community, from which he drove to his office in the heart of New York City. He traveled a great deal and was often away from home over the weekend.

"My executive responsibilities are heavy," Roger told Dr. Gray, "and I live on a very tight schedule. My wife resents my being away from home so much. She complains that I neglect her and the boy, and we bicker frequently. I can't get these aggravations out of my mind, and my work suffers. My worries don't add up to much, but probably some professional advice would help me manage better."

After a few individual interviews, Roger was asked if

he would like to talk over his problems with other clients, some of whom had similar concerns. He accepted the recommendation to join a new group being formed at the center by Dr. Gray.

"In the first session, Roger seemed surprised that I gave no directions," Dr. Gray continued. "He asked several times what the members were supposed to do, and what would go on. He was accustomed to formal agendas. In his opinion, meetings got nowhere unless there were rules of procedure which were made clear in advance. 'You would like rules,' I told him. 'You want to know how to work in this group, and you feel that rules are necessary.' That response, you probably know, is characteristic of my general approach. I paraphrase the counselee's statements without expressing approval or disapproval. I show interest in whatever he says and accept it unquestioningly. I operate on the assumption that he will eventually work out the solutions to his problems himself. I don't ask questions, give advice, or pronounce judgments."

A woman in Dr. Gray's group responded to Roger's statement by saying that she didn't consider rules very important; she could talk about her own difficulties without being given directions. He listened intently to her and to the other counselees, asking a few questions from time to time about their disclosures but giving little information about himself.

After five or six sessions, Roger said that he was accustomed to organized discussions with specific objectives in mind. He was a disciplined person; even as a child he'd never had time to float around. It would be more difficult for him to operate as he was expected to in this group; but if the others could manage it, so could he. He proceeded to talk about his executive tasks, explaining how he planned the activities of his subordinates. Various questions were put to him about his work by the other members of the group. One of them commented that he had risen very quickly in his firm and must be very able and efficient. Roger reported that he was feeling better generally, but he was apparently becoming more and more uncomfortable during the sessions.

A few weeks later, he expressed anxiety about the absence of direction in the group. He felt lost without rules, as fearful as a disobedient child. He recalled a memory of himself, at the age of five, lying alone on the sidewalk screaming and kicking. His mother had left him there in a tantrum to continue her shopping. After talking about this memory with a great deal of emotion, Roger spoke frankly about his parents: a rigid demanding woman married to a man given to violent outbursts of temper. To disobey or disappoint them had made him feel threatened and insecure.

"He lived up to his parents' expectations by making a brilliant scholastic record and getting ahead fast in business, he said, but he never learned how to play," Dr. Gray declared. "In the group he found that people were accepted when they operated without specific direction, and this put him again on his mettle to conform. It was a hard lesson, but now he behaves in a much more relaxed way. He feels secure about being spontaneous. The non-directive approach breeds spontaneity."

The climate of understanding and safety created by Dr. Gray's procedure impressed Dr. Louis Steeple as being similar to that which developed in his own analytically conducted groups. Their members were not put under any pressure to conform, and were encouraged by his own neutral attitude to talk freely about their experiences. Apart from the fact that the non-directive therapist did not go beyond conveying the essence of his client's statements whereas the analytically oriented therapist made interpretations, what other differences were there in the two approaches, Dr. Steeple asked.

There were many basic differences, in Dr. Gray's opinion. "I don't conduct an investigation of the past life of the group member or direct his mind into particular channels. I don't apply psychoanalytic principles of transference and resistance. Memories come up, as I have just illustrated, but the group members are not asked to produce them and they are not an important aspect of the group process. My clients talk about whatever they please because they get to feel safe with each other and accepted by me. The counseling experience is designed to help them move forward by scrutinizing and changing their own attitudes and finding their own solutions to their problems. I regard myself as a catalyst of growth rather than a healer."

"Roger was rigid and overcontrolled when he started," said Wanda Green. "Obviously, he obtained a great deal of emotional release in your group. What experience have you had with the opposite type of personality? Won't an over-impulsive person run wild in such an atmosphere?"

"Sometimes he tries to rule the roost at first," Dr. Gray replied. "Eventually he identifies in his behavior with the more constrained members. Their attitudes put a damper on his impulsivity."

"I gather that the unconscious doesn't get much emphasis in the non-directive system," Dr. Steeple remarked.

"I don't deliberately focus on unconscious processes," Dr. Gray asserted, "but the kind of group structure I have described brings out a great deal of emotion. In that sense, I actually am studying what you call the unconscious."

Asked for further information about Roger, his counselor said that it was too soon to evaluate the results in this case. The man was already more relaxed, freer emotionally; he would probably be much more comfortable after another six months in the group. He might also need some individual counseling to work out his family problems.

Dr. Gray was asked to give another illustration of his own interventions. He replied: "In one session Roger was silent until an incident related by another client reminded him of one of his own experiences as a boy of eight. His father, in a fit of rage, picked up a chair and hurled it across the room. Roger said he looked at the remains of the chair and wondered if his father would crush him in the same way. He ran to his mother. Instead of reassuring him, she ordered him to pick up the pieces of the chair. I told him: 'You are saying that your father behaved violently and that your mother was very demanding.' I spoke without emotion and I did not go beyond reflecting the gist of his statement. I did not explain the connection between Roger's memory and his present situation."

"In an analytic interpretation," Dr. Steeple said, "Roger might have been informed that he had not been talking in previous sessions because of his fright and tension. He would have been told that it reminded him of the fright and tension he experienced in his own home as a child."

I was asked to give my impressions of Dr. Gray's case. I pointed out that Roger was a man with both business and family problems who tended not to participate at the beginning of his group experience. Eventually, however, through his own communications and those of the other group members, he developed intense emotions, which led to the recall of highly significant emotional experiences with his parents. The opportunity to express his feelings about them without meeting with censure or rebuff was beneficial to him. He got the impression that the group accepted him and was concerned primarily with helping him understand his own behavior. No demands were made on him to talk; this, too, was helpful. Since he was not threatened with expulsion for refusing to talk, his anxiety was reduced. He was less tense and had more energy for his work.

"People have various kinds of difficulties getting into treatment," I added. "Initially, they are less resistant to one form than to another. If, for example, a person was subjected to a great deal of discipline and domination and deeply resented it, or if he longs for freedom from certain immediate responsibilities, he may find the climate of a non-directive group very appealing. However, it may take some time for him to adjust to it."

"It would be interesting to hear how a case of this sort would be handled through another procedure," Miss Green remarked. "For example, through family counseling. That's what Jack Bush does. Maybe he'd tell us how he would respond if Roger approached him for help with the family problems Dr. Gray just mentioned."

"That will require some imagination, but I'll try to give you a general idea," said Dr. Bush, a man in his thirties who exuded energy and optimism. "I'd like to have a few more facts about Roger's wife and son."

"My memory is at your disposal," Dr. Gray responded. "Roger has described his wife, Ernestine, as a pretty woman who gave up a promising career in merchandising to marry. She has resented being tied down by her household responsibilities and the absence of congenial neighbors. She appears to be an overanxious mother. Their son, Ted, is a well developed boy for his age who chafes at his mother's restrictions and his father's neglect. Ted has trouble getting up in the morning and frequently misses the school bus."

"Let's assume that Roger came to the consultation center and psychiatric clinic where I work," Dr. Bush began. "I should explain that its various programs are based on the treatment philosophy and methods of Alfred Adler and his followers. On Roger's first visit, he would have been interviewed by a social worker; she would have taken a detailed personal and family history. The case might then be referred to me following a diagnostic study, or family counseling might be used as an exploratory procedure. In either case, Roger would have been enrolled with his wife and son. All three would come to the center for a series of sessions spaced several weeks apart. While I counseled Roger and Ernestine with a few other couples in the counseling room, Ted would be in another room playing with other children under observation."

Dr. Bush continued his account: "The playroom supervisor would report to me on the boy's behavior in the course of the session, and later I would call him to the counseling room for a brief interview. His parents would be out of the room while I talked with the youngster, but the other parents would remain and take part in the discussion. They would also talk over the family's problems with Roger and Ernestine on their return to the consulting room. Then I would express my own opinions and counsel them. This sounds like an elaborate operation; I suppose it is. The family is first alerted to the nature of its problems and then it is helped in a common-sense way to weld itself into a co-operative unit."

He maintained direct control and lectured at times during counseling sessions, Dr. Bush explained, but parents were encouraged to think out solutions to their own problems together. Their individual preoccupations were pointed out to them in the group, and later in private sessions.

"Now let's get back to our case," Dr. Bush went on. "Roger and Ernestine would both be asked in the first session to give their impressions of their difficulties and air their grievances about each other's attitudes. For example, Roger might complain that Ernestine was bringing Ted up improperly and couldn't get him out of the house in the morning. When he missed the school bus, Roger had to drive him to school, which meant getting late to the office. Ernestine harassed him every day by telephoning about trivial matters; in the evening, he was much too tired to go out again or to be bothered by his wife and son. He was a good provider. Wasn't that enough?

"I would call on Ernestine to reply to these charges. She would lodge the countercharge that Roger behaved like a guest in his own home. My interview with Ted would probably make it clear that he was adversely affected by his parents' preoccupations and chronic quarrels. He might identify with his father's attitude and express resentment over his mother's nagging and insistence that he stay in his own back yard when he wanted to play with a chum just three blocks away."

In the later counseling sessions, husband and wife would report how things were going and cite evidence of changes for the better in the home situation. Dr. Bush went on: "I would have explored with Roger his attitude that people nowadays don't work hard enough. I suspect that he'd eventually admit that the excessive demands of his job were largely self-imposed. Had he gone to the office last weekend or had he readjusted his schedule? I would hope to hear that he'd bought Ted the baseball glove the boy had asked for, and that they had played together last Saturday. How many times a week did the three of them have dinner together? In brief, were they being motivated to change their attitudes and were they working out a better plan of family living? We would familiarize them with our conviction that co-operative parents have co-operative children. The child who is a problem to his parents may be a child with problem parents."

When Dr. Bush had finished, Doris Bacon, another member of the discussion group, raised a crucial issue. "Shouldn't we consider the possibility that Roger might be unable to respond to practical advice? He seems to be a pretty sick man. At least, that's the impression I got from Dr. Gray's report."

"I mentioned that Roger would have been admitted to the counseling program only after a diagnostic study or to test out his suitability," Dr. Bush reminded her. "If it became evident that family counseling would not meet his needs, we would recommend that he enter psychotherapy. My basic assumption about the people I counsel is that they are capable of benefiting from guidance."

I suggested that the group keep in mind the different frames of reference of the counselor, the therapist, and the analyst. Each of them made a different assumption about his cases. I continued: "As Dr. Bush has just stated, he assumes that his counselees just need guidance, advice, and direction. The psychotherapist assumes that his patient or client needs assistance in improving his behavior or changing his attitudes. The analyst assumes that there are emotional obstacles to the patient's healthful functioning which have to be cleared away. By the way, the Pavlovians would say that he needs to undo the effects of bad conditioning through a process of deconditioning and reconditioning. As far as I can tell, none of us is a simon-pure operator, but our initial orientation to those who seek our help is determined by our respective frames of reference. We also know enough to refer cases not suitable for our procedure to someone who can handle them or, if necessary, for further psychiatric study.

"Occasionally this becomes necessary because the person who needs help doesn't necessarily select the kind he needs; he prefers the procedure which will be most comfortable for him. Who would want to be operated on for a brain tumor if a massage would cure it? Direct counseling such as the type just described by Dr. Bush often appeals to people who were neglected children. They are eager for advice and direction; they want to learn new ways to behave. This type of counseling may also be sought by a person who has a great fear of the unknown within himself and would rather not explore it.

"However, if he has deep-seated problems, he usually finds himself incapable of benefiting from counseling. It's good advice, he may say, but it won't work for me. If he tries to follow it, he will experience intolerable distress. This would be pretty clear evidence that he needed some so-called uncovering, disinhibiting, or deconditioning procedure. This would put him in control of feelings he was unaware of and eventually enable him to release them. The non-directive approach demonstrated by Dr. Gray enabled Roger to secure a great deal of emotional release. Those of you who employ the action or dramatic types of therapy know that these, too, free people of their inhibitions, at least temporarily."

"I'd like to get some information about psychodrama," said Dr. Gray. "My impressions of it are confused. I've heard contradictory descriptions."

"I don't doubt that." Dr. Harold Pine, a man with expressive features, smiled as he spoke. "The essence of psychodrama is spontaneity. No two situations are exactly alike.

Besides, there are many modifications of the classical psychodrama associated with Dr. Moreno. This is the form employed at the Psychodrama Institute and various large institutions, but it involves a large staff and elaborate staging. Simplified procedures are also used, with or without a stage. We conduct psychodrama at our agency for groups of about ten or twelve. I lead them with the help of a social worker and a few other staff members."

Wanda Green asked him to outline the development of a case in psychodrama. How would Dr. Pine have worked with Roger, for example, if he had sought such treatment?

"To help along this discussion, I'll imagine what he might experience," Dr. Pine replied in his deep voice. "In the course of a lively session covering many topics, he would have been invited to tell the story of his life to the group. As he did this, the current conflicts he was unable to cope with would come to light. Then these would be discussed by the group, and I would make my preparations to dramatize these conflicts during the next session. Roger would play himself. Other group members might volunteer to play the other roles in his personal drama, or I might assign them to members of the staff, possibly including myself. We would represent Roger's auxiliary egos—in other words, the people who figured significantly in his conflicts. I would set the scene, so to speak, and coach the players on how to project his problems but, when the time came, they would improvise their own lines.

"It seems likely that the auxiliary egos in this psychodrama would be Ernestine and Ted. We might dramatize one of their quarrels, maybe several of them. His wife would plead with Roger to do something for her, or to be a good father to Ted. The man would complain that she didn't appreciate how hard he worked all day. 'Don't bother me!' Roger might exclaim angrily. Ernestine would become distraught and Ted would misbehave. Anyway, that will give you a rough idea. Someone else might then re-enact the role of Roger while he watched; through this mirroring procedure, we would demonstrate to him what the other group members thought of his behavior."

A discussion usually followed one of these psychodramas, Dr. Pine explained. At this time other group members would express their opinions of Roger's problems; they might recommend solutions to him. Someone might point out that Ernestine and Ted might be less demanding if Roger gave them more attention or that other efficient executives managed to be good husbands and fathers. Between that session and the next, Roger would undoubtedly do a great deal of thinking about his difficulties. He would report his reactions and the results of his soul-searching to the group.

I said: "Psychodrama and similar procedures for the acting-out of sensitive life situations in a neutral atmosphere appeal to many emotionally deprived people who are unaware of their feelings. Some of them love the atmosphere of the drama. In addition to the spectacle itself, the support of the group and the sober discussion of their problems may lead to fresh insight as well as better modes of behavior. All who participate get new perspectives. This is true also of the play and activity group therapies for children. As you know, Miss Green works with youngsters in a guidance clinic. Maybe she'd be willing to explain what happens in her groups."

"Roger won't do for this demonstration, but I'll imagine that we were consulted about his son, Ted," Miss Green said. "He might be a good candidate for activity group therapy. At least, many of the boys accepted for activity groups have the same kind of behavior problems and anxiety that Ted seems to have. His first interview would give us the impression that he was very much under the thumb of a parent and that a socializing experience with other children in a tension-free atmosphere would benefit him. In the group he would bang things around, play games with the others, or do anything else he chose to do without adult interference. I observe and reply to questions but don't intervene unless the children become dangerously violent to each other or are likely to blow up the building.

"At first Ted would expect me to shush and control him; he'd be surprised at the amount of freedom he was permitted. The results of this experience would show up after a while at home and school. Of course, we'd solicit his parents' co-operation. Our attitude would be that his mother should permit him to spend more time with the kids in the neighborhood and that he needed more attention and guidance from his father."

"How do you work with adolescents?" Dr. Gray asked.

"They talk together," Miss Green explained. "Their groups are essentially the same as those for adults. Usually we treat adolescent boys and girls separately. Mixed groups create too much excitement. They do very well in these interview groups. I don't intervene in their discussions any more than necessary."

"Now that we're covering the age spectrum, I'd like to hear about Miss Bacon's work with the aged," Dr. Pine said. "Is it therapy or counseling?"

"We do both in what we call therapeutic social clubs," Miss Bacon replied, "but these clients benefit primarily from companionship and sympathetic understanding of their problems. They usually respond more slowly than younger people; but after ten or fifteen sessions, they begin to feel they're having a worth-while experience. They discuss common problems; feelings of being useless, unwanted, or in the way of in-laws often dominate their sessions. They benefit from listening and being listened to. They help each other develop healthier attitudes and find useful ways to spend their time."

"It occurs to me that we are a pretty good cross section of group practitioners," said Dr. Steeple. "We meet various kinds of human needs. Some of us give guidance and tell people how to improve their behavior. Others among us help them improve it. Still others try to undo damage caused by previous life experiences so that people will be free to behave in more desirable ways."

"But all of us start out in the same way," Miss Green declared. "We respond to what a person consciously perceives and identifies as his problem. If this does not turn out to be his basic difficulty, we make him aware of what it really is; but we all begin by dealing with the problem as he presents it."

"I agree with you," I told her. "The patient is always the primary source of our knowledge of his emotional disturbance. Directly and indirectly, he tells us what is wrong with him. We use our personalities in various ways to work with him on his problem. How we go about it is relatively unimportant; the important thing is to solve the problem."

The diversity of our approaches to this problem give rise to numerous explanations. One is that many different kinds of people seek professional assistance in dealing with emotional disturbances; and those who provide it are also differently constituted human beings. The other basic reason is that the causes and nature of these disturbances are still unknown. They are treated on the basis of theories—

assumptions—and these are varied. The methods generally employed today crystallize the assumptions that have proven to be valid for the treatment of mental illness.

Persons who feel the need for a therapeutic group experience usually drift into the type of group that most appeals to them. It arouses some emotion that can be developed in the treatment process. Age, temperament, social background, material resources, responsibilities, and various other circumstances influence their choice.

The diverse professional backgrounds, personal qualities and resources of those who render the various forms of psychological assistance are reflected in their commitment to a particular mode of treatment or counseling. They don't operate "out of a book"; theory blends with personality. Within the general framework of their respective methods, they usually function with considerable flexibility, devising responses consonant with their personal judgment, skill, and comfort.

When the members of my discussion group analyzed their procedures, they found out that they had more in common than they had recognized. They did not limit themselves to the techniques characteristic of their respective methods, but "borrowed" others as necessary to accomplish their immediate objectives. Despite the differences in their major emphases, the techniques they employed were often similar.

"I don't limit myself to interpretations," Dr. Steeple said. "At times I just reflect a group member's statement in a non-committal way, or mirror it back at him dramatically. I even give advice at times, though I'm not interested in whether it's followed. I give it to study the reactions to it."

Some of the divergences in the methods themselves seemed to diminish under close scrutiny. It was pointed out, for example, that the more intensively and extensively the non-directive therapist or counselor applied himself to the emotional problems of his group members, the closer he came to the analytic approach. Eventually, the differences between those two methods would be almost indistinguishable.

Good functional results are secured in most cases through all of the group methods. Some types of groups are better than others at particular stages of treatment, though this varies from person to person. The resolution of the basic problem in a case may be resolved through any of the methods, or it may be relieved only temporarily. If the patient is not helped sufficiently, or cannot sustain the benefits of his first group venture, he may continue his treatment in another type of group or in a private relationship. None of our methods is consistently effective.

We are concerned today not only with curing our patients but also with learning the most efficient way to do it—the least costly in time, money, and effort. The learning process is facilitated by the analytic method to a much greater extent than the other approaches employed. The application of the psychoanalytic theory of personality development to observations based on the method of treatment derived from that theory provides us with much more information on how a person became ill, how his illness developed, and the precise reparative experience he requires.

It is becoming increasingly clear that, in any course of treatment, the development of an emotional relationship which produces feelings of health and maturity is the essential curative factor. Each of the methods employed provides a different set of keys to unlock those feelings. It is my impression that we will eventually be able to create a few master keys that could be wielded comfortably and effectively by all of the persons who treat or counsel, on behalf of all of those who need their services. After we have learned how to use these master keys efficiently, we may discard some of our present ones. Until then, however, all of our present keys may prove to be indispensable.

[I I]

Looking Ahead

"I'D RATHER BELIEVE that I was sick and the world was okay than that I'm getting well and the world is sick," a man recovering from a severe mental illness said recently. "Then I'd know that everything would be fine when I got better. This way it's a lot harder. I wish I knew what was ahead of me. Will I be able to stay well in such a sick world?"

To make this a healthier world, I told him, all sorts of obstacles would have to be cleared away: from the undesirable attitudes of parents to threats of thermonuclear warfare. But coping with a sick world was a dilemma which faced many people recovering from illness. He, too, would have to face the unknown and create his own solution. I could not give him the security of knowing what the future would bring him.

He might have enjoyed this security had he lived in ancient Greece and consulted one of those oracles or diviners whose remarkable predictions we become familiar with in our schooldays. They had a genius for summing up in a few cryptic words the destiny of every person who turned to them. Wisest of all, perhaps, was Tiresias, the blind seer who prophesied the doom of Oedipus and Narcissus and the happier fate in store for Ulysses. In a few unadorned phrases, Tiresias faithfully predicted the outcome of personality tendencies which a psychoanalyst must study for many hours before he understands their significance.

The art of prophecy has been crippled by the sciences of human behavior. In ancient times man was bound to whatever emotional tendencies developed in him early in life; although he couldn't do much about them, he could find out where they would propel him by consulting a prophet. But today man is no longer forced to move in that direction. We have learned how to alter his early emotional currents or influence him to rise above them. Hence, it is harder to foretell the precise direction in which he is moving, individually or collectively.

In the field of mental healing, magic and omniscience have given way to knowledge, but how it will grow and benefit us in the future is difficult to predict. In psychotherapy especially, we usually meander far beyond the range of our present understanding and influence, and envisage what lies ahead in terms of our ultimate objectives. Perhaps this will help us shape things in the present so that we will have the kind of future that we would agree was desirable.

The two psychotherapeutic sciences about which I have written opened up at the start of my own lifetime. When I was a student they were not included in the curriculum of the medical school. It has taken another thirty years for them to begin to gain the recognition of academic medicine. But both of these sciences are still crude; their bodies of theory and practice have yet to emerge from infancy.

These developments of one lifetime represent no more than a few days in the history of mankind's struggle to understand and conquer mental illness. Within these broader dimensions, it was only yesterday when Freud introduced the idea of listening to a patient's free associations in the privacy of the doctor-patient relationship and Pratt started to listen to his patients in a group. Today and tomorrow we shall have to continue to refine both of these hearing-aids and improve our skills in using them. Only then will we get to know their real potentialities.

A decade or so ago, their relative effectiveness was a controversial issue. The majority of psychotherapists lined up in two opposing camps. One believed that group treatment was an expedient fad, the other that the days of individual psychotherapy were numbered. The debate continues, but views as extreme as these are rarely voiced today.

Meanwhile, we have to learn how to use both forms of treatment with more precision. Our choice of one or the other is still based largely on personal preference and convenience. For instance, most of the patients I place in groups have had some individual treatment; I transfer them to the other setting, or use both simultaneously, when I have the impression that a group experience will make some further contribution to their welfare. Some psychotherapists start patients in a group and complete their treatment in the other setting. We have as yet no detailed study of comparative results to guide us in making our selections. The accurate delimitation of the respective shortcomings and values of the two settings is a task for the future.

The most intensive individual psychotherapy involves five

or six hours of treatment a week. No group treatment of equal intensity has been reported. Groups usually meet once or twice weekly, for a total of from one and one half to four hours. To determine the relative efficiency of the settings for specific conditions, the results achieved in one case through five hours of individual treatment weekly would have to be compared with the progress of six persons in group therapy thirty hours a week.

In view of the great strides which have been made in group treatment of far less intensity, I believe that the results of such a study would startle those who now regard it as the less efficient method of obtaining information from people and getting to understand them. There is no question in my mind that it would turn out to be the more powerful treatment instrument, though not the more effective for *all* types of emotional disturbances. In certain cases it will not serve as a substitute for the tête-à-tête, any more than a father and siblings can give an infant the same kind of emotional nurturing as a mother. Undoubtedly, the more intimate relationship will continue to be the essential therapeutic agent for the corrective reliving of the earliest experiences in life.

In other words, the contours of the psychotherapy of the future are clear. It will be combined treatment. Both individual and group therapies will continue to be administered, but more scientifically and skillfully than they are at present.

Today we know much more about the constructive use of our procedures—psychotherapeutics—than about their destructive potentialities. These will undoubtedly command more attention. A psychological communication which benefits a person in one "dosage" may be harmful to him in a larger dosage or to someone else in the original dosage. Eventually the undesirable reactions to our words and attitudes will be studied much as the undesirable reactions to drugs are studied in general medicine and pharmacology. As we gain more understanding of these reactions, I anticipate the development of a science of *toxipsychology*, corresponding to toxicology. Just as the latter science alerts the physician to the harmful dosages and undesirable applications of drugs and other medicine, toxipsychology would provide safeguards against the toxic usages of psychological procedures.

Group treatment is now conducted primarily as a co-operative venture for strangers. With their entry into treatment, each of them joins a group to which he has never belonged in the past. Actually, it is an artificial group which exists only for the purpose of treatment, in contrast to the numerous other groups to which its members belong or have belonged in the past. But group psychotherapy will shortly encompass the joint treatment of people who are related in life, especially those who are biologically related —a family. The direct treatment of other "natural" groups in their own settings is also in the offing. In fact, a few therapy groups have already been formed in the public schools.

To treat a group of strangers requires more skill than treating one person; but to treat a family is even more demanding. Such treatment is already under way on an experimental basis, along with family diagnosis.

Growing interest in the family as a unit in diagnosis and treatment reflects the knowledge we have acquired, both through group therapy and the investigations of social scientists, about the effects of family interaction on the health of its members. Studies of family living patterns which promote emotional disturbances are being conducted by research psychiatrists [1] and appear to be culminating in systems of family diagnosis and therapy, as well as in educational programs for the improvement of family life. Meanwhile, practitioners experienced in group psychotherapy occasionally consider it advisable to treat the members of a family together. I find myself doing this with increasing frequency.

The trend toward family treatment is easy to explain. Most problems which bring people into psychotherapy are connected with their early family experiences. The rapid social, economic, and technological changes of this era, as well as two world wars, have weakened the structure and transformed the living patterns of many families. Undercurrents of tension and disharmony create the kind of home climate which helps to precipitate mental illness. The breakdown, treatment, and even the recovery of one person often upsets the equilibrium of his whole family. In such cases, observation and treatment of the family as a unit may be more effective than the individual treatment of the member who is originally identified as the patient.

A sad commentary on the prevalence of strife in family living today is my own unsuccessful search, over a period of years, for a painting of a happy family to hang in my waiting-room. The theme of the happy mother and infant has inspired many artists, but, as far as I can determine, no one has spontaneously painted a mother, father, and their offspring in a felicitous mood. "Our own experiences wouldn't suggest such a subject," one artist told me. The

[1] Outstanding contributions have been made by Dr. Nathan W. Ackerman of New York and Dr. John P. Spiegel of Boston. Their concepts and others developing in this field are presented in the report of a conference sponsored by the New York Academy of Medicine. See: Iago Galdston, Editor: *The Family in Contemporary Society* (New York: International Universities Press; 1958).

growing concern of scientific investigators with interaction
processes in the family circle appears to be justified.

Responsibility for the intellectual training of each new
generation has long been accepted by society, but it has
fallen down on the job of providing children with the
emotional training they need. When intellectual training
became too complicated for parents, it was taken over by
the schools. But the emotional training of the young is still
their parents' responsibility. The help they receive from
churches, youth organizations, and other agencies, though
valuable, is uncertain and limited. The present high inci-
dence of mental illness suggests that emotional education is
too difficult a task to be entrusted almost entirely to parents.
It is also too crucial a task, for each time they fail a child's
life is blighted. The time may not be far off when society
accepts the responsibility for emotional training and en-
trusts it to the schools.

The first move in this direction, which I have already
mentioned, was the introduction of group therapy into the
schools. But more is needed than treatment for children
who have undergone some damaging experience. Therapy
ought to be supplemented by groups and classes in emotional training for all children beginning with their ad-
mission to public or private schools.

Teaching them how to handle their feelings is as important, in my opinion, as teaching them how to work with
letters and figures and other intellectual concepts. They
need to understand why they feel angry, melancholy, or
tearful at times and what is healthful and socially appropriate for them to say and do in these states. The desirability
of thinking and talking about troublesome feelings and the
undesirability of discharging them in asocial behavior are

lessons which every person should learn early in life. The distinction between the "sayable" and the "doable," so vital for emotional health, is one which many adults have to be taught today in the course of psychotherapy. Emotional education at an early age would obviate the need for such re-education. Children can learn how to discharge their energy in personally and socially useful ways. Proper instruction makes it second nature for them to behave accordingly and pleasurable enough so that they don't want to behave in other ways.

As time goes on, we shall get to know much more about the curative factors in psychotherapy than we do at present. It was originally believed that what healed a patient was the lifting of his repressions, through the recall of memories. Then we came to recognize that what was important was not the memories but what had prevented their recall. The integration of the ego and the achievement of insight were subsequently identified as the decisive factors. At the present time we tend to concentrate on emotional communication, learning problems, and the unlearning of old behavior. In the next decade or so, I expect that we shall define the treatment process as one of helping people "grow up"— that is, of providing them symbolically, through words and attitudes, with the emotional ingredients which they failed to obtain in their early development.

Psychoanalysts have "talked around" this concept for some time, but we still know practically nothing about the ingredients to be provided. For example, how much gratification and frustration, love and hatred, rest and activity does a person require in his formative years to move from one stage of psychological development to the next? We know that each human being has different needs, but we have yet to establish norms and variations. These should enable us to determine the precise sequence and dosages of emotional ingredients which would permit a patient to complete the cycle of human maturation—in other words, to satisfy his maturational needs.

Eventually, I believe that we will know as much about creating the emotionally mature personality as we now know, say, about the breeding and growing of flowers. These are fastidiously controlled operations in a greenhouse which observes the principles and rules laid down by plant geneticists and pathologists. From the selection of seeds and soil to the daily care of the blooms throughout the course of their growth, nothing is left to chance. The well-trained horticulturist knows how much sunlight and shade, moisture and fertilizer are required by each of his products. He carefully protects them from insects and wind-blown pollen, from fungi and viruses. Ingenious devices at his disposal overcome inhibitions or retardations in growth encountered by the flowers he nurtures. The breeder of new varieties knows how to control color and size, the length of stems, and the structure of petals. The flowers produced through such methods are hardier and superior in appearance to those grown haphazardly.

We are not able to cultivate a personality as thoughtfully today because the science of human maturation has scarcely developed. Our knowledge of the psychological needs of the human organism is still extremely limited. The mother's body provides it with a sheltered environment for nine months; but birth exposes it to all sorts of eventualities. If it incurs significant damage in the course of its emotional growth on home soil, sooner or later it may have to be transplanted to a controlled environment: the psychotherapeutic setting. This is about the only greenhouse we have on this earth for human beings. The psychotherapist tries to repair the damage and provide whatever is needed to ripen the personality.

Though this is, at best, a patch-up job, it permits us to make detailed studies of the responses of the personality to the regrowth processes. The studies are made with a view to perfecting the operations of the greenhouse itself. These observations also provide valuable source material through which we should eventually be able to identify the emotional experiences which are essential at each phase of growth to produce the mature personality.

Our immediate objective is to learn what these experiences are and to provide them with the utmost efficiency through combined treatment—individual and group psychotherapy. Once we have perfected these procedures, however, I believe that the knowledge and skills acquired in healing emotionally damaged individuals will be applied to rearing them in a non-damaging way. How to utilize this knowledge to improve the health of society as a whole we shall learn in some measure from group psychotherapy.

Today this whole field appears to be in a stage of transition. Representatives of the various schools are already borrowing from each other. While concepts and techniques developed by non-analytic practitioners are being incorporated into analytic group psychotherapy, the non-analytic therapies are being permeated with psychoanalytic principles and terminology. It is my impression that group treatment is evolving into the psychoanalysis of groups. This would be based fundamentally on present concepts of transference and resistance and employ not only interpretation, to which classical psychoanalysis is generally limited, but whatever additional techniques have been developed to effect basic changes in the personality and enable it to mature.

Healing is a by-product of the psychoanalytic method. Its explicit goal is the acquisition of knowledge about emotional processes. However, knowledge for the sake of knowledge is a "luxury" we cannot always afford in view of the pressing need for treatment. As this need is substantially reduced through the proper emotional education of oncoming generations, groups will be oriented increasingly to the promotion of understanding. In a healthier age, people will enter groups to learn why their minds operate as they do when they function together. The science of group psychoanalysis will help us find ways of growing, living, and working more healthfully and peacefully in natural groups.

Social scientists have learned a great deal about spontaneous behavior in natural groups, especially in the family, the work team, and the youth gang. We know that people talk and conduct themselves very differently in therapy groups; but the dynamic processes operating in the latter groups constitute an almost untouched field of research. We don't yet know, for example, how the presence of persons with specific psychiatric disorders influences a group's functioning or the merits of various possible combinations of patients. Studies of natural groups give us some clues on behavior in therapy groups and suggest fruitful areas of research, in order to deepen our understanding of why people function as they do in groups formed for therapeutic purposes.

On the other hand, one may reasonably anticipate that group psychoanalysis will provide knowledge which can be utilized to improve the functioning of natural groups.

We expect to find out how conflicting emotional states and changes in the distribution of mental energy disorganize behavior. Studies based on group-treatment experiences which approximate as closely as possible the experience of an individual in psychoanalysis would increase our understanding of the psychological needs which cause people to function unevenly or inefficiently in natural groups; we shall also learn how these needs should be dealt with to improve their functioning. The controlled environment of group psychoanalysis would provide ideal conditions for observing how various types of social experiences contribute to personality disorders and how those suffering from them, in turn, contribute to the deterioration of life in the community.

Group psychoanalysis would also demonstrate how these disorders and social stresses can be avoided. Patients engaging simultaneously in the process of emotional evolution would work out constructive approaches to the conflicts which commonly arise in community life and explore various ways of adjusting themselves to its ever-changing realities. As they prove that modes of behavior which safeguard emotional well-being also enable people to contribute in larger measure to the general welfare, society will recognize that maximum productivity and therapeutic living are equally desirable goals and mutually compatible processes. The concept of mental illness as a product of unhealthy living will pervade society, and our concern will gradually shift from the treatment of individual cases of illness to programs to raise the general level of wellness.

The ultimate task of the psychotherapist will be to eliminate the need for his services. Just as diphtheria, smallpox, and other dreaded diseases have been conquered through vaccines, improved sanitation, and other preventive measures, diseases which respond to psychological treatment will eventually cease to be medical problems. In the course of time these conditions will yield to social and educational programs, to be conducted through the home, the school, industrial enterprises, and other community settings.

It is the responsibility of the psychotherapist to find out what prophylactic measures are needed and how they may be applied. This is what he is now learning, in co-operation with his allies: the patients who lie on his couch or sit in his therapy circle.

A Note about the Author

HYMAN SPOTNITZ was born in Boston in 1908. After graduating from Harvard University in 1929, he went on to receive his M.D. from the Friedrich Wilhelms University, Berlin, in 1934, and his MED. SC. D. from the College of Physicians and Surgeons, Columbia University, in 1939. He then started upon a career in neurology and psychiatry, which took him as a resident and research worker to the Neurological Institute and the New York State Psychiatric Institute, as assistant neurologist to the Vanderbilt Clinic and Columbia University, and as an adjunct psychiatrist to the Hospital for Joint Diseases and Mount Sinai Hospital. Drawn into group therapy through his work as Consultant Psychiatrist at the Jewish Board of Guardians, he is now recognized as one of the outstanding teachers of group techniques and principles. He continues to engage in the private practice of both individual and group psychotherapy.

This is Dr. Spotnitz's first book, although he has contributed chapters on group therapy to various professional books, including *Specialized Techniques in Psychotherapy* (1952) and *The Practice of Group Therapy* (1947), and is the author or co-author of more than fifty published papers on psychoanalytic psychiatry, group psychotherapy, and neurology. Dr. Spotnitz lives in New York City with his wife and three sons.

January 1961

A Note on the Type

THE TEXT of this book was set on the Linotype in Janson, a recutting made direct from the type cast from matrices long thought to have been made by Anton Janson, a Dutchman who was a practising type founder in Leipzig during the years 1668–87. However, it has been conclusively demonstrated that these types are actually the work of Nicholas Kis (1650–1702), a Hungarian who learned his trade most probably from the master Dutch type founder Dirk Voskens.

Composed, printed, and bound by
KINGSPORT PRESS, INC., Kingsport, Tenn.
Paper manufactured by
P. H. GLATFELTER Co., Spring Grove, Pa.
Typography and binding design by
VINCENT TORRE

PUBLIC LIBRARY

SEP 5 1961

STOCKTON, CALIF.